BIBLICAL

BABY GIRL NAMES FROM GENESIS TO REVELATIONS

BY COLIN WALLACE

Biblical Baby Girl Names From Genesis to Revelation

Copyright © 2026 by Colin Wallace

Published by:
Christ Day By Day Media Inc.
www.christdaybyday.com

Disclaimer

This book is a work of research, interpretation, and devotional reflection. While the author and publisher have made every effort to ensure the accuracy and completeness of information contained in this book, we assume no responsibility for errors, inaccuracies, omissions, or any inconsistency herein. The interpretations of biblical texts, names, and historical contexts are those of the author and are intended for inspirational and educational purposes. Readers are encouraged to consult primary biblical translations, scholarly commentaries, and original language resources for personal study.

All efforts have been made to trace and properly attribute copyright holders of quoted material. The publisher welcomes being brought into contact with any copyright holders not here acknowledged so that appropriate corrections may be made in future editions.

Printed in the United States of America

ISBN 979-8-90329-351-3 PAPERBACK
ISBN 979-8-90329-356-8 HARDCOVER
ISBN 979-8-90329-354-4 EBOOK

INTRODUCTION 6

NAMES FROM GENESIS TO DEUTERONOMY 13

WOMEN OF ACTION AND INFLUENCE: GENESIS TO DEUTERONOMY 24

CONCEPTUAL AND DESCRIPTIVE NAMES FROM GENESIS TO DEUTERONOMY 36

HEROINES OF FAITH AND COURAGE - JOSHUA TO ESTHER 46

QUEENS AND FIGURES OF COURT - JOSHUA TO ESTHER 64

NAMES FROM THE POETIC BOOKS - JOB TO SONG OF SOLOMON 77

NAMES FROM THE PROPHETIC BOOKS - ISAIAH TO MALACHI 86

NAMES FROM THE FAMILY OF JESUS 94

NAMES OF WOMEN TRANSFORMED BY CHRIST 103

NAMES OF SISTERS IN THE EARLY CHURCH 131

THINGS TO CONSIDER : CARRYING THE STORY FORWARD 149

APPENDICES 156

INDEX OF NAMES (ALPHABETICAL) 156

INDEX OF NAMES BY BIBLICAL BOOKS 174

BIBLIOGRAPHY 192

ABOUT THE AUTHOR 193

INTRODUCTION

The First Breath, The First Word

Imagine the moment. Dust swirls in a sunbeam, newly formed, still hanging in the air. The divine breath animates clay, and the first human draws its first, shuddering breath. In that pristine silence, before any other word of relationship or command is spoken, God speaks a name. He calls this new being 'Adam' —from the earth, of the earth. Soon after, from the side of this earth-being, another is drawn forth. And to her, the man speaks his first recorded words: a poem, and within it, a name. "She shall be called Ishah," he says, "for she was taken out of Ish (man)." But then, in a more intimate act of understanding, he names her personally: Chavah, "Eve"—the mother of all living. Before the story truly begins, before the plot of humanity unfolds into tragedy and redemption, we are given this foundational truth: to be known is to be named, and to be named is to be called into a story.

From that Genesis dawn to the final "Amen" of Revelation, the Bible is a book saturated with names. It is not merely a chronicle of events but a tapestry of identities. Mountains, cities, altars, and, most profoundly, people are named, their designations carrying the weight of destiny, memory, prophecy, and grace. A name in Scripture is rarely just a phonetic tag for convenience. It is a condensed biography, a spoken prophecy, a memorial of God's intervention, or a parent's deepest hope or sharpest sorrow. To know the name is to begin to know the story, and to know the story is to glimpse the character of the God who authors it all.

This book is an invitation to walk through that grand, sprawling narrative once more, but with a specific, intimate focus: the names given to girls and women. From the famous matriarchs to the nearly forgotten daughters, from historical figures to symbolic representations, we will listen for the echo of these names. Why? Because in a world where ancient texts can sometimes feel distant, and where choosing a name can feel overwhelming in its modernity, there is a profound connection to be found in these ancient syllables. To name a child Sarah, Deborah, or Mary is not merely to select a pleasant sound from an old book. It is to consciously tether her life to a specific strand of a cosmic story—a story of faith wrestled in the dark, of courage that defies empires, of loyalty that redeems families, and of grace that transforms the unlikeliest of souls.

The Terrain of a Name: Identity, Heritage, and Blessing

In our contemporary, globalized world, names often function differently. We might choose a name for its aesthetic appeal, its uniqueness, or its familial tradition. These are beautiful reasons. But in the ancient Near Eastern and Mediterranean contexts that birthed the Bible, a name was understood to be intrinsically connected to the essence of the person or thing it identified. A name was thought to encapsulate the core nature of its bearer.

This is why God's names are so critical: El Shaddai (God Almighty), Yahweh Yireh (The Lord Will Provide), Yahweh Rapha (The Lord Who Heals). Each reveals an aspect of His character and His relationship with His people. Similarly, the changing of a name marked a fundamental shift in identity and destiny. Abram ("Exalted Father") becomes Abraham ("Father of a Multitude"). Jacob ("Heel-Grabber," Supplanter) becomes Israel ("He Struggles with God"). Saul ("Asked For") becomes Paul ("Small"). The new name declares a new reality ordained by God.

For women, this power of naming was equally potent, though often reflected through a different social lens. A daughter's name could be:

A Theological Declaration: Hannah means "grace" or "favor," and her life becomes a testament to God's gracious answer to desperate prayer.

A Historical Marker: Zipporah ("bird") may reflect her Midianite heritage or a hoped-for characteristic.

A Prophetic Statement: The prophet Hosea is commanded to name his daughter Lo-Ruhamah ("Not Loved"), a devastating living symbol to Israel of their broken covenant.

An Expression of Circumstance: Leah ("weary") is given a name that seems to foreshadow her initial experience of being unloved.

A Legacy of Character: Dorcas (Greek) or Tabitha (Aramaic), both meaning "gazelle," is memorialized not for the animal's speed but for its grace—a fitting name for a woman "full of good works and acts of charity."

When we understand this, we see that to explore biblical names for girls is to explore the full spectrum of human experience before God: joy and sorrow, triumph and failure, faithfulness and rebellion, obscurity and renown. It is to recover stories that have sometimes been relegated to footnotes and to listen for the voices of women who, though often operating within the constraints of patriarchal societies, were indispensable agents in the story of salvation.

Why These Names Endure: Timeless Stories in a Single Word

The names in this book have survived the collapse of empires, the rise and fall of languages, and vast cultural shifts. They have journeyed from Hebrew tents and Roman villas to 21st-century birth certificates. Their endurance is a mystery worth pondering. I believe it rests on three pillars.

First, these names are rooted in authentic, often gritty, human stories. The Bible is no hagiography of perfect people. Sarah laughs in disbelief and then, in jealousy, casts out her rival. Rebekah masterminds a deceitful scheme to secure her favorite son's future. Rachel steals her father's idols. Yet, each is woven into the lineage of the Messiah. Their names carry not the sterile perfume of perfection, but the rich, fertile soil of real life—faith mingled with doubt, love with jealousy, courage with fear. This makes them relatable. To name a daughter Rachel is not to wish upon her a life of petty theft, but to connect her to a narrative of passionate love, deep yearning, and ultimate inclusion in God's plan despite human flaws.

Second, these names connect us to archetypal virtues and vocations. Deborah ("bee") evokes the image of industry, community, and, when provoked, a fierce sting. She was a prophetess, judge, and military leader—a name for a woman of wisdom and decisive action. Ruth ("friend," "companion") is the eternal emblem of loyal love (chesed) that chooses commitment beyond reason. Mary (from Miriam, "bitterness" turned "beloved") represents ultimate surrender and discipleship. Lydia ("from Lydia") reminds us of the strategic role of hospitable hearts and open homes in spreading the faith. These names become shorthand for virtues we wish to cultivate and legacies we hope to leave.

Third, and most importantly, these names are landmarks in the story of God's redemptive work. They are not random. Each woman, named or unnamed, plays a part—sometimes central, sometimes peripheral—in the great narrative arc from Creation to New Creation. From Eve, the mother of all life and the one through whom the promise of a redeemer (the "seed") is first whispered, to the woman of Revelation 12, clothed with the sun and giving birth to the Messiah, female figures bookend and populate the story. They are integral, not incidental. To choose a biblical name is, therefore, to consciously place your child's identity within this oldest and grandest of stories—the story of a Creator's love, a creation's fracture, and a long, patient, costly work of redemption.

How to Walk Through This Book: A Guide for Your Journey

This book is designed as both a reference and a narrative journey. It is for the expectant parent poring over lists late at night, for the student of theology curious about the women of the early church, for the novelist seeking authentic period names, and for anyone who simply loves the stories of Scripture and wants to know the people within them more deeply.

We will travel in canonical order, from Genesis to Revelation. This is not because it is the only way, but because it allows us to feel the sweep of the story. We will watch how names and their contexts evolve from the patriarchal tents of Canaan to the royal court of Persia, from the fishing villages of Galilee to the cosmopolitan ports and house churches of the Roman Empire.

For each name, we will explore:
1. The Name Itself: Its original language (Hebrew, Aramaic, Greek), its phonetic beauty, and its core meaning.
2. The Story in Scripture: A recounting of the biblical narrative in which she features. Who was she? What were her circumstances, her choices, her triumphs, and her struggles?
3. The Cultural & Historical Context: What would her world have been like? What can archaeology, history, and sociology tell us about the life of a woman in her time and place?
4. The Spiritual Legacy: How does her story reveal God's character or advance His redemptive plan? What enduring virtues, warnings, or hopes does her life embody?
5. The Name Today: Considerations for modern use, including potential nicknames, middle-name pairings, and the distinctive legacy the name now carries.

We will also pause to consider the profound silence that surrounds the unnamed women—the daughter of Jephthah, the woman with the issue of blood, the Samaritan woman at the well. Their anonymity in the text is itself a kind of story, reminding us that God's notice and grace extend far beyond the recorded names.

A Name as a First Prayer

Finally, consider this: in many traditions, the act of naming a child is one of the first and most sacred duties of a parent. It is, in essence, a foundational prayer spoken over a new life. You are speaking an identity into the space between you, the child, and God. When that name is drawn from the well of Scripture, that prayer becomes layered with millennia of faith.

To name your daughter Abigail ("My Father's Joy") is to pray that she will know she is the delight of her Heavenly Father. To call her Esther ("Star") is to pray she will shine with courage and wisdom in dark times, for "such a time as this." To choose Anna ("Grace") is to pray her life will be marked by a patient, expectant faith that recognizes the Savior. Even names born in hardship, like Leah or the pre-transformed Miriam ("bitterness"), can be redeemed in the telling, becoming testaments to how God brings beauty from ashes and transforms our stories.

This book, then, is more than a catalog. It is an invitation to wander through the family album of faith. It is a chance to meet your spiritual ancestors, to hear their stories anew, and to consider how you might extend their legacy into the future. As you turn these pages, may you listen for the echo of these names—not as distant historical artifacts, but as living words, still speaking, still calling, still blessing. May you find here not just a name, but a story. And in that story, may you find a prayer for the life just beginning.

Let us begin where the story begins: in a garden, with the first breath, and the first name.

1.
NAMES FROM GENESIS TO DEUTERONOMY

The Mothers and Matriarchs of the Pentateuch: Genesis to Deuteronomy

The foundational books of the Bible are framed by the stories of patriarchs—Abraham, Isaac, Jacob, and Moses. Yet, moving silently and powerfully alongside them are the matriarchs, women whose faith, decisions, struggles, and encounters with God were indispensable to the formation of the nation of Israel. Their names, echoing through millennia, carry the weight of promise, the sting of pain, and the quiet assurance of divine providence. Here, we explore these founding mothers in the order they entered the story.

Eve (Chavah)

Original Language & Core Meaning: Hebrew: חַוָּה (Chavah). Derived from the root chayah (חָיָה), meaning "to live" or "to breathe." Her name means "Life" or "Living One," and Adam explicitly states, "because she was the mother of all living" (Genesis 3:20).

Biblical Narrative: Eve is the first woman, created from Adam's side ("bone of my bones, flesh of my flesh") as his ezer kenegdo —a helper corresponding to him, a powerful term often used for God as Israel's helper. Placed in the perfection of Eden, she engages with the serpent, is deceived, eats the forbidden fruit, and shares it with Adam. This act introduces sin, shame, and brokenness into creation, resulting in exile from the garden. Her punishments involve multiplied pain in childbirth and a strained dynamic with her husband. Yet, in the midst of judgment, God gives her the first gospel promise: her "seed" will one day crush the serpent's head (Genesis 3:15). She becomes the mother of Cain, Abel, Seth, and "other sons and daughters."

Cultural & Historical Context: In the ancient Near East, creation stories often depicted humans as afterthoughts or slaves to capricious gods. The Genesis account is revolutionary: humanity is the pinnacle of creation, made in God's image, with woman sharing equally in that divine imprint and purpose. Her formation from the man's side signifies equality and intimate partnership, not superiority or inferiority.

Spiritual Legacy & Redemptive Role: Eve is the mother of all humanity, both in life and in the inheritance of a sin nature. Her story reveals the devastating consequences of disobedience and the fracture of relationships (with God, each other, and creation). More importantly, she becomes the first bearer of the Protoevangelium —the first promise of a Redeemer. The "seed of the woman" who will crush evil initiates the entire redemptive arc of Scripture, culminating in Jesus Christ, born of a woman (Galatians 4:4). Her name, "Life," looks forward to the One who is the Resurrection and the Life.

Modern Use:

Usage: A classic, short, and profoundly meaningful name. It has shed much of its purely "first woman" association to feel both vintage and sleek.

Nicknames: Evie is the overwhelmingly popular and sweet diminutive.

Middle Name Pairings: Eve serves beautifully as a first or middle name. Pairings often balance its simplicity: Charlotte Eve, Eleanor Eve, Genevieve Eve, Lydia Eve. As a first name: Eve Alexandra, Eve Catherine, Eve Josephine, Eve Magnolia.

Sarah (Originally Sarai)

Original Language & Core Meaning: Hebrew: שָׂרָה (Sarah), originally שָׂרַי (Sarai). Sarai is believed to mean "My Princess" (with a possessive suffix). Sarah means "Princess" or "Noblewoman" universally. The change signifies her move from being Abraham's princess to a princess of nations.

Biblical Narrative: Sarah is the wife of Abraham and central to the covenant promise. She is beautiful, strong-willed, and pragmatic. Her profound struggle is decades of barrenness in a culture where offspring defined a woman's worth. In desperation, she gives her Egyptian servant, Hagar, to Abraham, leading to the birth of Ishmael and enduring family conflict. At 90 years old, she overhears the divine promise of a son and laughs in disbelief. Yet, God is faithful, and she bears Isaac ("He Laughs"), the child of promise. She later secures Isaac's inheritance by insisting Abraham send Hagar and Ishmael away. She dies at 127 in Hebron.

Cultural & Historical Context: A woman's primary role was to produce heirs. Barrenness was seen as a divine curse and a personal shame. Sarah's actions with Hagar were legally sanctioned by contemporary customs (seen in the Nuzi tablets), where a barren wife could provide a surrogate. Her laughter at the divine message reflects the utter human impossibility of the promise.

Spiritual Legacy & Redemptive Role: Sarah is a pillar of the faith narrative (Hebrews 11:11). Her story demonstrates that God's promises are fulfilled not by human ingenuity (the Ishmael scheme) but by divine power (the birth of Isaac). The covenant line, through which the whole world will be blessed, passes through her. She is a model of eventual belief and a key figure in establishing the lineage of the Messiah. Her new name marks her central role in God's royal, redemptive plan.

Modern Use:

Usage: A perennial favorite, Sarah has been a top name for centuries. It conveys grace, classic beauty, and strength.

Nicknames: Sadie (originally a diminutive of Sarah), Sally, Sara.

Middle Name Pairings: Sarah Elizabeth, Sarah Grace, Sarah Juliette, Sarah Vivian. As a middle name: Abigail Sarah, Eleanor Sarah, Hannah Sarah, Lydia Sarah.

Rebekah (Rivkah)

Original Language & Core Meaning: Hebrew: רִבְקָה (Rivkah). The etymology is uncertain; popular theories connect it to the root rbq, meaning "to tie" or "to bind," or to a word for "ensnaring beauty." Thus, "To Bind" or "Captivating."

Biblical Narrative: Rebekah's story begins at a well, where she displays remarkable kindness and vigor by watering Abraham's servant's ten camels. She willingly leaves her family to marry the unseen Isaac. After 20 years of barrenness, Isaac prays for her, and she conceives twins who struggle in her womb. God tells her, "the older shall serve the younger." She favors Jacob, the younger, and masterminds the deception to secure Isaac's blessing for him, orchestrating the theft of Esau's birthright. This forces Jacob to flee, and she never sees him again.

Cultural & Historical Context: Her betrothal story follows a common ancient type-scene (the meeting at the well). The custom of the father's blessing was irrevocable and carried the weight of a legal will. Rebekah's manipulative actions, while morally complex, can be seen as an attempt to ensure the outworking of the divine oracle she alone had received.

Spiritual Legacy & Redemptive Role: Rebekah is an active, decisive instrument in God's plan. Her story reveals that God's sovereign election often works through deeply flawed human motives and actions. The promise (the younger over the older) is upheld not through human virtue but through divine providence that oversees even deception. She is a crucial link, ensuring the covenant passes to Jacob (Israel).

Modern Use:

Usage: Rebekah (and the Rebecca spelling) is a classic that feels both biblical and literary. It suggests intelligence, determination, and beauty.
Nicknames: Becky, Becca, Reba, Riva.
Middle Name Pairings: Rebekah Anne, Rebekah Charlotte, Rebekah Faye, Rebekah Sophia. As a middle name: Elise Rebekah, Grace Rebekah, Julia Rebekah, Natalie Rebekah.

Leah (Le'ah)

Original Language & Core Meaning: Hebrew: לֵאָה (Le'ah). Likely derived from a root meaning "to be weary" or, alternatively, from the Akkadian word for "cow" (littu), a symbol of fertility. Thus, "Weary" or "Wild Cow."

Biblical Narrative: Leah is thrust into a marital deception, given to Jacob in place of her younger sister Rachel. Described as having "weak eyes" (possibly tender or delicate), while Rachel was beautiful. Jacob loves Rachel and works another seven years for her. Leah is unloved, yet God "opens her womb," and she bears six sons (Reuben, Simeon, Levi, Judah, Issachar, Zebulun) and a daughter (Dinah). Her naming of her children chronicles her heartache and hope for her husband's affection (e.g., Judah means "I will praise the Lord"). She ultimately finds her worth not in Jacob's love but in her role as a mother, particularly of Judah, the royal and messianic line.

Cultural & Historical Context: In a polygamous society, rivalry between co-wives for affection and status through childbearing was intense and painful. Leah's situation was one of profound humiliation and loneliness.

Spiritual Legacy & Redemptive Role: Leah's story is a profound testament to God's compassion for the unloved and overlooked. He sees her affliction and bless her with fertility. Her life demonstrates that God's purposes are often advanced through those the world deems less worthy. Crucially, the Messiah, Jesus, comes from her son Judah's line, not from Rachel's favored son Joseph. Redemption flows through the line of the "unloved" wife.

Modern Use:

Usage: Leah has enjoyed consistent popularity. It feels gentle, strong, and grounded.
Nicknames: Lee, Lea.
Middle Name Pairings: Leah Beatrice, Leah Caroline, Leah Margaret, Leah Rose. As a middle name: Amelia Leah, Chloe Leah, Olivia Leah, Sophia Leah.

Rachel (Ra'chel)

Original Language & Core Meaning: Hebrew: רָחֵל (Ra'chel). Means "Ewe" —a female sheep. In the pastoral context, this signifies value, gentleness, and beauty.

Biblical Narrative: Rachel is the beloved, beautiful shepherdess Jacob meets at a well. He works seven years for her, only to be given Leah. He works seven more years for her. She remains barren for years, leading to desperate envy of her sister. She cries to Jacob, "Give me children, or I shall die!" She eventually bears Joseph, who becomes Jacob's favorite, and later Benjamin, dying in childbirth on the road to Bethlehem. Her stolen household idols and her father Laban's search for them remain a mysterious episode in her story.

Cultural & Historical Context: Her barrenness, contrasted with Leah's fertility, was a deep source of shame. The theft of the household gods (teraphim) may have been an attempt to claim legal rights to family inheritance.

Spiritual Legacy & Redemptive Role: Rachel represents the deep human longing for love and fulfillment. Her story shows that even being the beloved wife does not shield one from profound suffering. Her tears are remembered prophetically (Jeremiah 31:15) as the weeping of Israel in exile. Yet, from her beloved son Joseph comes the preservation of the family in Egypt, a crucial step in forming the nation. Her burial near Bethlehem creates a geographical link to the future Messiah's birthplace.

Modern Use:

Usage: An enduringly popular name, Rachel evokes beauty, kindness, and a touch of melancholy grace.

Nicknames: Rae, Chelley, Shelly.

Middle Name Pairings: Rachel Emily, Rachel Jane, Rachel Louise, Rachel Victoria. As a middle name: Audrey Rachel, Eleanor Rachel, Hannah Rachel, Katherine Rachel.

Conclusion of the Matriarchal Line

These five women—Eve, Sarah, Rebekah, Leah, and Rachel—form the core matriarchal line. Their intertwined stories of hope, despair, faith, and manipulation are not clean morality tales but raw accounts of God working His perfect will through imperfect people. They teach us that God hears the cry of the barren (Sarah, Rachel), sees the pain of the unloved (Leah, Hagar), and weaves even human deception (Rebekah) into His sovereign plan. Their legacies culminate in the twelve tribes of Israel and, ultimately, in the coming of Jesus Christ, the promised "seed" who crushes the serpent and blesses all nations. Their names, when spoken today, still carry the echo of that ancient, unfolding promise.

2. WOMEN OF ACTION AND INFLUENCE: GENESIS TO DEUTERONOMY

The foundational books of the Bible, Genesis through Deuteronomy, are often viewed through the lens of the patriarchs—Abraham, Isaac, Jacob, Joseph, and Moses. Yet, woven intricately into and often determining the course of their narratives are women of profound action, influence, and faith. Their stories, set against the backdrop of a nomadic, patriarchal, and covenantal world, reveal a God who sees, hears, and works through all people—men and women alike—to advance His redemptive plan. Here, we explore these women chronologically, from the Garden to the Plains of Moab.

הָגָר (Hagar)

Original Language & Core Meaning: Hebrew, likely of Egyptian origin. Possibly "Flight" or "Immigrant."

Biblical Narrative: An Egyptian servant of Sarah, given to Abraham as a concubine. When she conceives, she looks with contempt on her mistress, leading to harsh treatment and her flight into the wilderness. By a spring, "the Angel of the Lord" (a theophany) finds her, commands her return, and promises her innumerable offspring through Ishmael (Genesis 16). Years later, after Isaac's birth, she is cast out with her son. In despair in the desert of Beersheba, God again hears Ishmael's cry, reveals a well to her, and reiterates His promise (Genesis 21:8-21).

Cultural & Historical Context: Hagar occupied the lowest rung: a foreigner, a slave, and a concubine. Her story exposes the harsh realities of household power dynamics. Her encounters in the desert highlight the precariousness of life for a single woman and child without tribal protection.

Spiritual Legacy & Redemptive Plan: Hagar is the only person in Scripture to name God: El Roi, "the God who sees me" (Genesis 16:13). Her narrative is a profound testament to God's care for the marginalized, the outcast, and the foreigner. While the covenant line runs through Isaac, God makes a separate, gracious nation from Ishmael because of His care for Hagar.

Modern Use:

Popularity: Rare but growing, appreciated for its strong biblical and multicultural resonance.

Nicknames: Aggie, Hari.
Middle-Name Pairings: Hagar Noor, Leila Hagar, Hagar Ruth, Naomi Hagar.

דִּינָה (Dinah)

Original Language & Core Meaning: Hebrew. "Judgment" or "Vindicated."

Biblical Narrative: The daughter of Jacob and Leah (Genesis 30:21). Her story (Genesis 34) involves her "going out to see the women of the land," where she is seized and violated by Shechem, a Hivite prince. Shechem then falls in love and seeks to marry her. Her brothers Simeon and Levi deceitfully agree on condition of circumcision, then slaughter all the men of the city, leading to Jacob's condemnation of their violence.

Cultural & Historical Context: Dinah's story is a brutal case study in tribal honor-shame dynamics and ancient sexual politics. Her violation was an offense against the entire clan's honor. The brothers' vengeance, while excessive, was understood in the context of tribal justice, where there was no higher legal authority. Dinah herself is a silent subject, her voice and fate unrecorded.

Spiritual Legacy & Redemptive Plan: Dinah's story reveals the destructive consequences of sin—both personal and collective—and the cycle of violence that plagues a fallen world. It sets the stage for the curse on Simeon and Levi (Genesis 49:5-7) and highlights the need for a just rule of law, which would later be provided in the Mosaic covenant.

Modern Use:
Popularity: Uncommon but distinctive.

Nicknames: Di, Dee, Dina.
Middle-Name Pairings: Dinah Rose, Claire Dinah, Dinah Pearl, Lucy Dinah.

תָּמָר (Tamar) – (Judah's Daughter-in-Law)

Original Language & Core Meaning: Hebrew. "Palm Tree," a symbol of dignity, resilience, and fruitfulness.

Biblical Narrative: Married successively to Judah's wicked sons, Er and Onan, both of whom die. Promised to the younger Shelah but not given, she takes matters into her own hands. Disguising herself as a cult prostitute (qedesha), she tricks Judah, her father-in-law, into fulfilling his levirate duty. When her pregnancy is discovered, she is nearly executed but produces Judah's seal, cord, and staff as proof. Judah declares, "She is more righteous than I" (Genesis 38).

Cultural & Historical Context: The levirate marriage custom (Deuteronomy 25:5-10, codified later) ensured lineage and care for a widow. Judah's failure endangered Tamar's survival. Her daring action, while shocking, was a desperate bid for justice and security within the bounds of the clan's understood obligations.

Spiritual Legacy & Redemptive Plan: Tamar's story is a scandalous but crucial thread in the messianic line. Her son, Perez, is the direct ancestor of King David and Jesus Christ (Matthew 1:3). Her narrative demonstrates God's grace working through deeply flawed human systems and righteous desperation to preserve the chosen lineage.

Modern Use:
Popularity: Unique and strong, with a beautiful natural meaning.

Nicknames: Tammy, Tam.
Middle-Name Pairings: Tamar Joy, Ruth Tamar, Tamar Grace, Esther Tamar.

אָסְנַת (Asenath)

Original Language & Core Meaning: Egyptian. Likely "She belongs to (the goddess) Neith" or "Gift of the Sun-god."

Biblical Narrative: The Egyptian wife given to Joseph by Pharaoh (Genesis 41:45). She is the mother of his two sons, Manasseh ("God has made me forget") and Ephraim ("God has made me fruitful"), whom Jacob later adopts as his own, granting them tribal status (Genesis 48).

Cultural & Historical Context: The marriage was a political act, integrating Joseph into the Egyptian aristocracy. Asenath was likely a high-status Egyptian, perhaps a priestess's daughter. Her marriage to a Hebrew slave-turned-vizier was extraordinary.

Spiritual Legacy & Redemptive Plan: Asenath represents God's providential care for Joseph and the embedding of the covenant family in a foreign land. Through her, the tribes of Manasseh and Ephraim are born, with Ephraim later becoming a dominant tribe in the Northern Kingdom. She signifies the inclusive, expansive nature of God's plan.

Modern Use:
Popularity: Very rare, exotic and historically rich.

Nicknames: Senna, Asa.
Middle-Name Pairings: Asenath Pearl, Lily Asenath, Asenath Rose.

שִׁפְרָה וּפוּעָה (Shiphrah & Pu'ah) – The Hebrew Midwives

Original Language & Core Meaning: Hebrew. Shiphrah: "Beauty" or "Clarity." Pu'ah: "Splendid" or "Girl."

Biblical Narrative: Two midwives who defy Pharaoh's genocidal order to kill all Hebrew male newborns. They "feared God" and let the boys live, telling Pharaoh the Hebrew women were too vigorous and gave birth before they arrived. God "dealt well" with them and gave them families (Exodus 1:15-21).

Cultural & Historical Context: As midwives, they held a respected, professional role. Their defiance was an act of civil disobedience at great personal risk. Their clever response to Pharaoh uses a stereotype of Hebrew vitality as a cover, a classic example of the "trickster" motif used by the powerless against power.

Spiritual Legacy & Redemptive Plan: These women are the first recorded resisters in the Exodus story. Their courageous, God-fearing act directly allows for the survival of Moses and an entire generation. They demonstrate that faithfulness to God supersedes allegiance to tyrannical authority, setting the stage for national deliverance.

Modern Use:

Popularity: Extremely rare. Puah is virtually unused; Shiphrah is unique.

Nicknames: Shippy, Pua.
Middle-Name Pairings: Shiphrah Hope, Mercy Shiphrah, Puah Joy.

יוֹכֶבֶד (Yocheved) – Jochebed

Original Language & Core Meaning: Hebrew. "Yahweh is glory."

Biblical Narrative: The mother of Moses, Aaron, and Miriam. To save her infant son from Pharaoh's decree, she places him in a waterproofed basket in the Nile reeds, with his sister Miriam keeping watch. She is later employed to nurse her own son after Pharaoh's daughter finds him (Exodus 2:1-10; 6:20).

Cultural & Historical Context: Her act was one of desperate ingenuity. The "ark" (tevah) she uses is the same word as Noah's ark, a vessel of salvation. Being paid to nurse her own son was a subversive gift of providence, allowing Moses to be raised with a foundational Hebrew identity.

Spiritual Legacy & Redemptive Plan: Jochebed's faith is cited in Hebrews 11:23. Her actions preserved the life of the deliverer. She represents the quiet, strategic faith of mothers who trust God with their most precious gifts, shaping the future of redemption from within the heart of the enemy's camp.

Modern Use:

Popularity: Rare, primarily in Jewish communities.

Nicknames: Joci, Coby.
Middle-Name Pairings: Jochebed Ruth, Miriam Jochebed, Jochebed Faith.

מִרְיָם (Miriam)

Original Language & Core Meaning: Hebrew. Etymology debated, possibly "Bitterness," "Rebellion," or "Wished-for Child." Linked to the Egyptian word for "Beloved."

Biblical Narrative: The prophetess and sister of Moses and Aaron. As a girl, she orchestrates Moses' rescue (Exodus 2:4-8). After the crossing of the Red Sea, she leads the women in a song and dance of victory (Exodus 15:20-21). Later, she and Aaron challenge Moses' unique authority and are punished with temporary leprosy, before being restored after Moses' intercession (Numbers 12). She dies in Kadesh (Numbers 20:1).

Cultural & Historical Context: Miriam held a recognized leadership role as a prophetess, a rare and esteemed title. Her song is one of the oldest pieces of poetry in the Bible. Her challenge to Moses reflects internal power struggles within the leadership structure of the new nation.

Spiritual Legacy & Redemptive Plan: Miriam is a foundational female leader in Israel. Her prophetic song establishes the pattern of celebrating God's saving acts. While disciplined for pride, she is forgiven and restored, illustrating God's correction of even key leaders. Micah 6:4 lists her alongside Moses and Aaron as a deliverer sent by God.

Modern Use:

Popularity: The form "Mary" is quintessentially classic; "Miriam" is a strong, traditional choice.

Nicknames: Mimi, Miri, Mitzi.
Middle-Name Pairings: Miriam Joy, Hannah Miriam, Miriam Rose, Grace Miriam.

צִפּוֹרָה (Tzipporah) – Zipporah

Original Language & Core Meaning: Hebrew. "Bird," "Little Bird," or "Spark."

Biblical Narrative: A daughter of Jethro (Reuel), the Midianite priest, and wife of Moses. She bears him two sons, Gershom and Eliezer. On the return journey to Egypt, she performs a startling and urgent act of circumcision on one of their sons to avert God's wrath against Moses, declaring, "Surely you are a bridegroom of blood to me!" (Exodus 4:24-26). She later rejoins Moses in the wilderness (Exodus 18:1-6).

Cultural & Historical Context: As a Midianite, Zipporah came from a nomadic tribe with its own religious customs. Her swift, decisive action in Exodus 4 suggests Moses had neglected the covenant sign of circumcision for his son, a serious omission for the new leader of Israel. Her act enforced the covenant, saving Moses' life.

Spiritual Legacy & Redemptive Plan: Zipporah's story highlights the absolute necessity of the covenant sign for those in the redemptive story, even when it seems strange or is neglected. She serves as an instrument of God's discipline and mercy, ensuring Moses fulfills his obligations before confronting Pharaoh.

Modern Use:

Popularity: Rare and distinctive.

Nicknames: Zippy, Zippi, Zora.
Middle-Name Pairings: Zipporah Jane, Ruth Zipporah, Zipporah Dawn.

בִּתְיָה (Bithyah) – The Daughter of Pharaoh

Original Language & Core Meaning: Hebrew. "Daughter of Yahweh." (A name given by the biblical author; her Egyptian name is unknown).

Biblical Narrative: The princess who discovers the baby Moses in the Nile basket. Recognizing him as a Hebrew child, she has compassion on him, defies her father's decree, and arranges for Jochebed to nurse him. She later adopts him as her son, naming him Moses ("Drawn Out") (Exodus 2:5-10).

Cultural & Historical Context: As a royal princess, she had the autonomy and resources to act counter to state policy. Her adoption of a foreign slave-child was an act of both compassion and significant risk.

Spiritual Legacy & Redemptive Plan: She is an instrument of divine providence, placing the future deliverer in the very palace of the oppressor, where he would receive the education and status needed for his future role. In 1 Chronicles 4:18, she is honored by name, and Jewish tradition holds she later converted to the worship of Yahweh.

Modern Use:
Popularity: Extremely rare.

Nicknames: Bith, Tiyah.
Middle-Name Pairings: Bithyah Grace, Hope Bithyah.

The Daughters of Zelophehad: מַחְלָה, נֹעָה, חָגְלָה, מִלְכָּה, תִּרְצָה (Mahlah, Noah, Hoglah, Milcah, Tirzah)

Original Language & Core Meaning:

Mahlah: "Sickness," "Weakness," or "Forgiveness."
Noah: "Motion," "Wandering," or "Rest."
Hoglah: "Partridge" or "To Dance in a Circle."
Milcah: "Queen" or "Counsel."
Tirzah: "Pleasantness," "Delight."

Biblical Narrative: These five sisters approach Moses and the assembled leaders at the entrance to the Tent of Meeting. Their father died without sons, and they petition for the right to inherit his property, lest his name be lost from his clan. Moses brings their case before God, who rules in their favor, establishing a new ordinance of inheritance for Israel (Numbers 27:1-11). The decision is later clarified regarding marriage within the tribe to keep the land (Numbers 36).

Cultural & Historical Context: Their request was legally and socially revolutionary. In a patrilineal society, land passed strictly from father to son. Their bold, public appeal to the highest authority was an act of great courage and love for their father's legacy.

Spiritual Legacy & Redemptive Plan: Their story is a landmark moment for justice and the elevation of women's status within the covenant community. It reveals a God who listens to the marginalized and adapts His legal structures to uphold righteousness and preserve the integrity of families. It underscores that God's law is a gift for human flourishing, not a rigid, impersonal system.

Popularity: All are very rare. Tirzah and Noah (for girls) have some modern usage. Milcah is antiquated.

Nicknames: Tirza, Millie, Hattie (for Hoglah).
Middle-Name Pairings: Tirzah Joy, Noah Grace, Mahlah Hope, Hoglah Faith, Milcah Ruth.

These women, from Eve to the daughters of Zelophehad, are not supporting characters in a man's story. They are co-participants in the grand drama of Creation, Fall, and the dawn of Redemption. Their names, meanings, and actions are essential threads in the tapestry of Scripture, revealing a God whose plan is advanced by all who, in faith and sometimes in desperate cunning, answer His call.

3.

CONCEPTUAL AND DESCRIPTIVE NAMES FROM GENESIS TO DEUTERONOMY

The names in this section are unlike the familiar Sarah or Rebekah. They are not the names of Israelite matriarchs, but of women whose identities are deeply entwined with the complex, often shadowed, narratives of the early biblical world—particularly the genealogies and encounters of the Edomites and Canaanites, the neighboring peoples of Israel. These names are often compound words or descriptive phrases that reflect the religious landscape, geographical realities, or social standing of their bearers. For modern use, they present a unique challenge and opportunity: they are strikingly beautiful, profoundly ancient, and carry narratives of a world both foreign and foundational. To choose one is to reach into the deep, archetypal soil of the Biblical story.

Aholibamah (אָהֳלִיבָמָה)

Original Language: Hebrew

Core Meaning: "My Tent is a High Place" or "Tent of the High Place"

Biblical Narrative: Aholibamah appears in the genealogy of Esau (Edom) in Genesis 36. She is listed as a daughter of Anah and a wife of Esau (Genesis 36:2, 25). Significantly, she is also noted as a "chief" or clan mother among the Edomites (Genesis 36:41, 1 Chronicles 1:52). Her children by Esau—Jeush, Jalam, and Korah—became Edomite chieftains. Her name stands in stark, evocative contrast to the narratives of the patriarchs. While Jacob's family sojourns with their altars to Yahweh, Aholibamah's very name is rooted in the Canaanite high places (bamot), the open-air shrines on hills where local deities were worshipped.

Cultural & Historical Context: In the Canaanite and broader Semitic religious practice of the 2nd millennium BCE, the "high place" (bamah) was a central feature of worship. It was a sanctified elevation, often featuring a stone pillar (massebah), a wooden pole (asherah), and an altar for sacrifices. A name meaning "My Tent is a High Place" suggests a person, and by extension a lineage, deeply connected to cultic authority or sacred space. It may indicate she was from a priestly family or that her tribe was known for guarding a prominent shrine. As an Edomite chieftainess, her name encapsulates the distinct, and from the Israelite perspective, rival, religious and cultural identity of Esau's descendants.

Modern Use:

Exceedingly rare. It is a name for a scholar, a historian, or parents deeply committed to unique biblical names. Its phonetic beauty (ah-HO-lee-bah-mah) is undeniable, with a rhythmic, lyrical quality. Potential nicknames could be Libby, Liba, or Olibia. Its use would be a conscious reclaiming of an ancient and powerful identity from a narrative often overlooked.

Basemath/Bashemath (בָּשְׂמַת)

Original Language: Hebrew

Core Meaning: "Fragrance" or "Spice" (from the root b-s-m, related to balsam).

Biblical Narrative: The name Basemath is borne by two distinct women in Genesis, causing some textual confusion.

1. Basemath, daughter of Elon the Hittite: She is the first named wife of Esau, mentioned in Genesis 26:34. Her marriage caused grief to his parents, Isaac and Rebekah, because she was a Canaanite woman.

2. Basemath, daughter of Ishmael and sister of Nebaioth: In Genesis 36:3, she is listed as another wife of Esau, taken by him after seeing his parents' disapproval of his Canaanite wives. She is the mother of Esau's son, Reuel.

The duplication may reflect different tribal traditions or scribal variations, but both women are connective tissue in the biblical genealogical map—linking Esau to the Hittites and to his own Ishmaelite kin.

Cultural & Historical Context: "Fragrance" was a profound luxury in the ancient world. Spices, perfumed oils, and incense were valuable trade commodities, symbols of wealth, hospitality, and divine favor. To name a daughter "Fragrance" was to wish upon her a life of delight, pleasure, and auspiciousness. It speaks to sensory appreciation and cultural refinement. That Esau married women with such names (the other being Mahalath, "Lyre") hints at his attraction to the established, cultivated Canaanite society, in contrast to Jacob's sojourning life.

Modern Use:

While not common, Basemath (and its variant Basmath) has a soft, vintage elegance. It fits with the trend of "word names" like Grace or Felicity, but with a more exotic, aromatic flair. The nickname Bas or Bess could make it more accessible.

Mahalath (מַחֲלַת)

Original Language: Hebrew

Core Meaning: "Lyre" (a stringed instrument) or possibly "Sickness/Disease" from a homonymic root. The musical meaning is strongly supported by its context.

Biblical Narrative: Mahalath appears in two brief references. In Genesis 28:9, Esau, realizing his Canaanite wives displeased his father, goes to Ishmael and marries Mahalath, the sister of Nebaioth. She is presented as a more acceptable wife from his extended family line. She is also likely the same person referred to as Basemath, daughter of Ishmael, in Genesis 36. The name also appears in the title of Psalm 53 (*"Upon Mahalath, a Maschil of David"*), indicating a known tune or musical style.

Cultural & Historical Context: Music was integral to ancient Near Eastern life—for celebration, mourning, liturgy, and royal ceremony. The lyre (kinnor) was the premier instrument. To name a daughter "Lyre" suggests a family of musicians, a hope for a life filled with music and joy, or an association with a specific song or ritual. Esau's choice of a wife named "Lyre" from the nomadic Ishmaelite tribe adds a layer of cultural nuance, challenging stereotypes about desert life being uncultured.

Modern Use:

A beautiful and melodic name with a direct artistic connection. It is unique without being incomprehensible. The "Molly" sound within it makes Molly a natural and charming nickname, bridging ancient meaning and modern familiarity.

Adah (עָדָה)

Original Language: Hebrew
Core Meaning: "Ornament," "Beauty," or "Morning."

Biblical Narrative: Adah is another wife of Lamech in the antediluvian genealogy of Cain (Genesis 4:19-20). She is the mother of Jabal (ancestor of tent-dwellers and herdsmen) and Jubal (ancestor of all who play the lyre and pipe). In the parallel genealogy of Esau (Genesis 36:2, 16), an Adah is listed as a daughter of Elon the Hittite and a wife of Esau. This Edomite Adah is the mother of Eliphaz and a grandmother of the Amalekites.

Cultural & Historical Context: As one of the earliest named women in the Bible, the Adah of Genesis 4 represents the dawn of human culture—her sons founding pastoralism and music. Her name, "Ornament," speaks to the human desire for adornment and aesthetic beauty, elements that define civilization. The Edomite Adah continues this theme, connecting the name to the founding of tribes. It is a name that evokes primal creativity and foundational identity.

Modern Use:

Simple, elegant, and vowel-forward, Adah fits contemporary naming trends perfectly. It is a recognizable alternative to Ada or Ava, carrying with it a deep, dual heritage of artistic creation and tribal matriarchy.

Zillah (צִלָּה)

Original Language: Hebrew
Core Meaning: "Shade," "Shadow," or "Protection."

Biblical Narrative: Zillah is the second wife of Lamech (along with Adah) in Genesis 4:19-23. She is the mother of Tubal-cain, the "forger of all instruments of bronze and iron," and Naamah, a rare named daughter in these early genealogies. Zillah is also the one to whom Lamech addresses his famous song of vengeful boasting, marking her as a witness to the rapid escalation of human violence and technological prowess.

Cultural & Historical Context: In the harsh climate of the Near East, "shade" is not a negative but a vital refuge from the lethal sun. It symbolizes protection, rest, and sanctuary. A name meaning "Shade" would be a blessing of safety and comfort. Zillah's role as mother to the first metalworker ties her line to a pivotal technological leap, while her daughter Naamah ("Pleasant") hints at the enduring human appreciation for beauty alongside power.

Modern Use:

Zillah has a sharp, stylish, and slightly mysterious sound. It aligns with names like Zara or Zella. Its meaning is universally positive and poetic, evoking images of coolness, peace, and shelter. The nickname Zilly or Zee could be used.

Naamah (נַעֲמָה)

Original Language: Hebrew
Core Meaning: "Pleasant," "Lovely," "Beautiful."

Biblical Narrative: Naamah appears only once in the Pentateuch, as the daughter of Lamech and Zillah and sister of Tubal-cain (Genesis 4:22). Her inclusion is notable simply because she *is* named among the early inventors and patriarchs. Later, in the Hebrew Bible, a Naamah is an Ammonite princess, wife of King Solomon and mother of Rehoboam (1 Kings 14:21).

Cultural & Historical Context: As one of the first women given a name meaning "Pleasant" or "Lovely," Naamah represents the enduring human valuation of grace and beauty amidst a narrative filling with violence and toil. Her presence suggests that even in the line of Cain, there was recognition of aesthetic virtue. The name is pure aspiration, a parent's hope for a daughter's agreeable character and life.

Modern Use:

Naamah is flowing, gentle, and deeply meaningful. It is more distinctive than Naomi but shares a similar soothing phonetic quality. It is entirely usable today, carrying a simple, timeless blessing of pleasantness.

Summary of Modern Viability:

Most Accessible: Adah, Naamah, Mahalath (with nn Molly). These blend well with modern tastes, are easy to pronounce, and have positive, clear meanings.

For the Bold & Scholarly: Aholibamah. A conversation-starter with immense historical gravity and poetic resonance.

The Elegant Choice: Basemath, Zillah. Offer distinct sounds and beautiful meanings ("Fragrance," "Shade") for parents seeking a name that is rare but not overly obscure.

Each of these names is a fossilized piece of a worldview, offering a daughter not just an identity, but a specific fragment of the ancient human story—from the first notes of music to the scent of spices, from the shelter of a tent to the height of a sacred mountain.

4.
HEROINES OF FAITH AND COURAGE - JOSHUA TO ESTHER

RAHAB (רָחָב)

The name Rahab (רָחָב) means "broad," "spacious," or "wide." In its verbal form, it conveys the sense of enlargement or expansion—a fitting name for a woman whose faith would expand beyond the confines of Jericho's walls to secure her place in Israel's genealogy.

Biblical Narrative: Rahab appears in Joshua 2 and 6. She was a Canaanite woman living in Jericho, described specifically as a זוֹנָה (zonah), a term that can mean either a prostitute or an innkeeper. When Joshua sent two spies to scout Jericho, they lodged in Rahab's house, which was built into the city wall. Alerted to their presence, the king of Jericho demanded she surrender them. Instead, Rahab hid the spies under flax on her roof and deceived the king's messengers, sending them on a false pursuit. In a profound theological confession to the spies, she declared: "The LORD your God, He is God in heaven above and on earth beneath" (Joshua 2:11). She bargained for the safety of herself and her family when Israel attacked. The spies agreed, instructing her to bind a scarlet cord in her window as a sign. When Jericho fell, Rahab and her family were spared. She later married Salmon, a prince of Judah, becoming the mother of Boaz and thus the great-great-grandmother of King David, placing her in the direct lineage of Jesus Christ (Matthew 1:5).

Historical & Cultural Context: As a resident of one of the oldest continuously inhabited cities in the world, Rahab was part of a sophisticated Canaanite urban culture that practiced polytheistic religion, often involving fertility rites and child sacrifice. Her profession, while socially marginal, may have given her a degree of economic independence and made her home a logical place for foreigners to seek lodging without suspicion. The scarlet cord echoes the blood of the Passover lamb in Egypt, marking her household for salvation amid judgment. Her inclusion in Israel and the Davidic/Messianic line demonstrates the radical inclusivity of Yahweh's covenant —extended not by bloodline but by faith.

Modern Use:

Rahab is a strong, historically rich name that has seen a resurgence among Christians drawn to her story of radical transformation and courageous faith. It carries a distinctive sound and powerful narrative weight.

Middle-Name Pairings:
- Rahab Elise (Elise: "pledged to God")
- Rahab Josephine (Josephine: "God will increase")
- Rahab Miriam (Miriam: "bitterness" or "beloved")
- Rahab Sophia (Sophia: "wisdom")

ACHSAH (עַכְסָה)

The name Achsah (עַכְסָה) likely derives from the Hebrew word for "anklet" or "bangle" (עֶכֶס, ekes), an ornament worn by women. It evokes beauty, adornment, and perhaps the tinkling sound of jewelry.

Biblical Narrative: Achsah appears in Joshua 15:16-19 and Judges 1:12-15. She was the daughter of Caleb, one of the two faithful spies who had believed God could give them the Promised Land. Caleb offered her in marriage to the warrior who would capture the city of Kiriath-sepher (Debir). His nephew Othniel took the city and won Achsah as his wife. After the marriage, Achsah approached her father with a request. She "urged" or "persuaded" him (the Hebrew suggests a strong, persuasive action) to give her an additional blessing. Having received the arid land of the Negev as her dowry, she asked, "Give me also springs of water." She demonstrated both discernment—knowing the land was useless without water—and the boldness to ask for what was needed to ensure her family's future prosperity. Caleb granted her request, giving her the upper and lower springs.

Historical & Cultural Context: Achsah's story unfolds during the violent, uncertain period of the Israelite conquest and settlement. As a woman in a patriarchal warrior society, her value was often tied to her role in forging alliances (as a prize for military success). Yet, the narrative highlights her personal agency. She was not a passive prize but an active participant who secured vital resources. Her bold request, made from a riding donkey (a symbol of status), reflects a confident woman who understood both her value to her father and the practical necessities of survival in a harsh land.

Achsah is an uncommon but beautiful name with a soft, melodic sound. It suits parents seeking a deeply biblical yet distinctive name that symbolizes discernment, courage, and the wisdom to ask for what is essential.

Middle-Name Pairings:
- Achsah Grace
- Achsah Noelle (Noelle: "Christmas," evoking gift and blessing)
- Achsah Brielle (Brielle: "God is my strength")
- Achsah Hope

DEBORAH (דְּבוֹרָה)

The name Deborah (דְּבוֹרָה) means "bee." In ancient Near Eastern symbolism, the bee represented industry, community, order, and sweet productivity, but also a potent sting when provoked.

Biblical Narrative: Deborah's story is told in Judges 4-5. She is unique in Scripture as both a נְבִיאָה (nevi'ah, prophetess) and a שֹׁפְטָה (shofetah, judge)—the only woman to hold the latter leadership role. She held court under the "Palm of Deborah" between Ramah and Bethel, where Israelites came to her for judgment. When the Canaanite king Jabin oppressed Israel with his formidable general Sisera and 900 iron chariots, Deborah summoned Barak from Naphtali. She delivered God's command to deploy troops at Mount Tabor, promising victory. Barak agreed only if Deborah would accompany him. She consented but prophesied that the honor of victory would go to a woman. Indeed, after Barak's forces routed Sisera's army, Sisera fled to the tent of Jael (see below), who killed him. Deborah's victory song (Judges 5), a masterpiece of ancient Hebrew poetry, celebrates God's deliverance and the crucial roles played by willing leaders and even the stars "from their courses" fighting for Israel.

Historical & Cultural Context: The period of the Judges (c. 1200-1050 BCE) was one of tribal fragmentation and cyclical apostasy. Deborah arose during a time of national crisis and male leadership failure (Barak's hesitation). Her authority as a prophetess and judge indicates that God's Spirit can empower anyone He chooses, regardless of gender, to lead His people. Her role did not overturn the patriarchal structure but operated powerfully within and through it in an extraordinary moment. Her story is one of political, military, and spiritual leadership combined.

Modern Use:

Deborah has been a consistently popular name in English-speaking countries since the mid-20th century, often shortened to Deb or Debbie. It carries connotations of wisdom, strength, and leadership.

Middle-Name Pairings:
- Deborah Ruth (Ruth: "friend, companion")
- Deborah Faith
- Deborah Louise (Louise: "famous warrior")
- Deborah Kate (Kate: "pure")

JAEL (יָעֵל)

The name Jael (יָעֵל) means "wild goat" or "ibex"—a sure-footed, agile mountain creature that symbolizes independence, survival in harsh terrain, and unexpected strength.

Biblical Narrative: Jael's story is interwoven with Deborah's in Judges 4:17-22 and celebrated in the Song of Deborah (Judges 5:24-27). She was the wife of Heber the Kenite, a clan related to Moses' in-laws who lived in peace with King Jabin. After Sisera's defeat, he fled on foot to Heber's tent, expecting asylum due to their political alliance. Jael met him, invited him in, covered him with a rug, and gave him milk. When he fell into an exhausted sleep, she took a tent peg and a workman's hammer and drove the peg through his temple into the ground, killing him. When Barak arrived in pursuit, she showed him the slain general. Deborah's song praises Jael as "most blessed of women," vividly recounting the act: "She put her hand to the tent peg and her right hand to the workmen's mallet; she struck Sisera; she crushed his head; she shattered and pierced his temple."

Historical & Cultural Context: Hospitality was a sacred, non-negotiable code in the ancient Near East. By inviting Sisera in, Jael assumed the duty of his protector. Her violation of this code was a shocking, scandalous act—but one interpreted by the biblical author as an act of holy violence against Israel's enemy. As a woman in a tent-dwelling society, the tools of her domestic sphere (peg and hammer) became instruments of deliverance. Her action fulfilled Deborah's prophecy and sealed Israel's victory.

Jael is a fierce, uncommon, and phonetically striking name. It appeals to parents looking for a powerful biblical name outside the mainstream, representing decisive action and unexpected agency.

Middle-Name Pairings:
- Jael Seraphina (Seraphina: "fiery, ardent")
- Jael Victoria (Victoria: "victory")
- Jael Simone (Simone: "God has heard")
- Jael Verity (Verity: "truth")

RUTH (רוּת)

The name Ruth (רוּת) likely derives from the Hebrew root רְעוּת (re'ut), meaning "friendship," "companionship," or "association." It embodies loyalty, devotion, and deep, covenantal love.

Biblical Narrative: The Book of Ruth is a complete novella set in the time of the Judges. A famine drove Elimelech, his wife Naomi, and their two sons from Bethlehem to Moab. The sons married Moabite women, Orpah and Ruth. After all three husbands died, Naomi decided to return to Bethlehem. She urged her daughters-in-law to stay in Moab. Orpah eventually agreed, but Ruth delivered one of literature's most beautiful pledges of loyalty: "Where you go I will go, and where you lodge I will lodge. Your people shall be my people, and your God my God" (Ruth 1:16). In Bethlehem, Ruth supported them by gleaning in the fields, providentially in the field of Boaz, a relative of Naomi's. Boaz, impressed by her character, showed her kindness and protection. Following Naomi's shrewd guidance, Ruth approached Boaz at the threshing floor to appeal to him as a kinsman-redeemer (go'el). Boaz honored her, redeemed the family's land, and married Ruth. They had a son, Obed, the grandfather of King David.

Historical & Cultural Context: As a Moabite, Ruth was from a nation often at odds with Israel, descended from Lot. Her status as a foreign widow placed her at the very bottom of the social and economic ladder—vulnerable and destitute. The story highlights the law of gleaning (Leviticus 19:9-10) as a social safety net and the custom of levirate marriage/ kinsman-redeemer (Deuteronomy 25:5-10) as a means of preserving a family line. Ruth's conversion to faith in Yahweh is central, and her inclusion in David's and Jesus's lineage showcases God's grace extending beyond ethnic boundaries.

Modern Use:

Ruth is a classic, timeless name that has never gone out of
fashion. It is simple, strong, and carries an immense legacy of
loyalty, kindness, and divine providence.

Middle-Name Pairings:
- Ruth Elizabeth
- Ruth Annalise (Annalise: "graceful oath")
- Ruth Caroline (Caroline: "free woman")
- Ruth Beatrice (Beatrice: "she who brings happiness")

HANNAH (חַנָּה)

The name Hannah (חַנָּה) comes from the Hebrew root חָנַן (chanan), meaning "grace," "favor," or "to be gracious." It signifies one who has received or embodies grace.

Biblical Narrative: Hannah's story opens 1 Samuel (Chapters 1-2). She was one of the two wives of Elkanah. Her rival, Peninnah, had children, but Hannah was barren—a source of deep anguish and social shame, exacerbated by Peninnah's taunting. During the annual pilgrimage to Shiloh, Hannah prayed fervently and tearfully at the tabernacle, vowing that if God gave her a son, she would dedicate him to God's service as a Nazirite all his life. Eli the priest initially mistook her silent, moving lips for drunkenness but, upon hearing her story, blessed her. God remembered Hannah; she conceived and bore a son, naming him Samuel ("God has heard"). True to her vow, after weaning him, she brought Samuel to Shiloh to serve under Eli. Her magnificent prayer of thanksgiving (1 Samuel 2:1-10) is a precursor to Mary's Magnificat, exalting God as the reverser of fortunes, the strength of the weak, and the sovereign ruler.

Historical & Cultural Context: In ancient Israel, a woman's primary value was often linked to bearing children, particularly sons to carry on the family line. Barrenness was seen as a divine curse or withholding of blessing. Hannah's story highlights the personal, emotional toll of this condition and the efficacy of earnest, personal prayer directly to Yahweh, even at a time when priestly corruption (Eli's sons) was rampant. Her vow was extreme—dedicating her only child to sanctuary service meant giving up the very thing that would have secured her social standing.

Hannah has been enormously popular since the late 20th century. It is a gentle, classic, and universally appealing name that carries a beautiful meaning and a story of heartfelt prayer answered.

Middle-Name Pairings:
- Hannah Joy
- Hannah Margaret (Margaret: "pearl")
- Hannah Claire (Claire: "clear, bright")
- Hannah Louise

ABIGAIL (אֲבִיגַיִל)

The name Abigail (אֲבִיגַיִל) is a compound: "My Father ('avi) is Joy (gil)." It suggests a source of paternal delight and, by extension, a woman of joyful character.

Biblical Narrative: Abigail's story is found in 1 Samuel 25. She was the intelligent and beautiful wife of Nabal, a wealthy but surly and foolish Calebite shepherd in Carmel. When David, then a fugitive from Saul, requested provisions from Nabal in return for his men's protection, Nabal insulted him. David vowed to destroy Nabal's household. A servant alerted Abigail, who acted swiftly and independently. Without telling her husband, she prepared a massive gift of food and wine and went to intercept David. With profound wisdom and diplomacy, she bowed before David, took blame upon herself, praised David's future as God's anointed, and persuaded him not to shed blood and incur guilt. David blessed her and heeded her. When she returned, Nabal was drunk at a feast. The next day, she told him what she had done, and he suffered a stroke and died ten days later. David then sent for Abigail to become his wife, recognizing her wisdom.

Historical & Cultural Context: Abigail acted with extraordinary agency within a dangerous patriarchal context. Her husband's folly had placed their entire household under a death sentence. Her intervention was a daring act of peacemaking that required courage, immense social intelligence, and theological insight (she uniquely identified David as the Lord's future prince). She navigated between the violent honor culture of the time and the higher calling of God's purposes. Her story is one of wisdom preventing disaster.

Modern Use:

Abigail is a perennial favorite, often shortened to Abby. It is seen as a sweet, strong, and intelligent name with a lovely meaning and a story of wisdom and decisive action.

Middle-Name Pairings:
- Abigail Rose
- Abigail Charlotte (Charlotte: "free man")
- Abigail Sophia
- Abigail Jane

THE WISE WOMAN OF TEKOA & THE WISE WOMAN OF ABEL BETH MAACAH

While not given personal names, these women hold the title חֲכָמָה (chachamah), "wise woman," a recognized role of counsel and mediation.

Biblical Narratives:

1. Woman of Tekoa (2 Samuel 14): Joab sent this woman to King David to persuade him to recall his exiled son Absalom. She pretended to be a grieving widow with a story about one son killing another and the clan seeking to kill her remaining heir. Her parable appealed to David's sense of justice and exposed his inconsistency in banishing his own son. David saw through the ruse but was moved by her wisdom, granting her request.

2. Woman of Abel (2 Samuel 20): During Sheba's rebellion, Joab besieged the city of Abel Beth Maacah. This woman negotiated with Joab from the wall, reminding him of Israel's tradition as a place of wise counsel. She then convinced the city elders to behead Sheba and throw his head over the wall, thus saving the city from destruction.

Historical & Cultural Context: These stories confirm that certain women in Israel held formal, recognized roles as wise counselors and negotiators. They functioned as diplomats and mediators, skilled in rhetoric and parable, and were trusted to engage with the highest levels of male leadership (the king, the general) to resolve crises. Their wisdom preserved life and restored peace.

Modern Use:

While not a given name, the concept inspires virtue. The Hebrew Chachamah ("wise woman") is occasionally used as a distinctive and meaningful name choice.

Middle-Name Pairings (if using Chachamah or the virtue "Wisdom"):
- Chana Wisdom (Chana: alternate form of Hannah, "grace")
- Sophia Chachamah (Sophia is Greek for "wisdom")
- Irene Wisdom (Irene: "peace")

ESTHER (אֶסְתֵּר) / HADASSAH (הֲדַסָּה)

Esther's Hebrew name was Hadassah (הֲדַסָּה), meaning "myrtle tree"—a beautiful, fragrant evergreen symbol of life, prosperity, and hope. Her Persian name, Esther (אֶסְתֵּר), is likely derived from the Persian word for "star" (setareh) or the goddess Ishtar, representing beauty and celestial guidance.

Biblical Narrative: The Book of Esther tells of a Jewish orphan, Hadassah, raised by her cousin Mordecai in the Persian diaspora during the reign of Xerxes (Ahasuerus). After the queen was deposed, Esther was taken into the king's harem and, following extensive preparations, won his favor to become queen, hiding her Jewish identity. When the virulently anti-Semitic Haman plotted to destroy all Jews in the empire, Mordecai appealed to Esther to intercede with the king—a perilous act, as approaching unsummoned could mean death. Mordecai's famous words spurred her: "And who knows whether you have not come to the kingdom for such a time as this?" (Esther 4:14). Esther called for a three-day fast among the Jews, then risked her life to approach the king. She was accepted and, through a series of strategic banquets, revealed Haman's plot and her own identity, leading to Haman's downfall, the salvation of the Jews, and the establishment of the feast of Purim.

Historical & Cultural Context: Set in the opulent, absolutist Persian court (c. 5th century BCE), Esther's story is one of diaspora survival. As a woman in the royal harem, she was in a gilded cage, subject to the king's whims. Her power was entirely indirect, exercised through beauty, wisdom, patience, and immense courage. The book is unique in the Bible for not mentioning God explicitly, yet His providence is evident in every "coincidence"—from the king's insomnia to Esther's timing. Esther's story is about using one's position, however precarious, to act for justice.

Esther is a vintage name that has returned to significant popularity. It is elegant, strong, and carries a sense of timeless grace and quiet heroism. Hadassah is also used, particularly in Jewish communities, and is the name of a major women's Zionist organization and hospital network.

Middle-Name Pairings:
- Esther Grace
- Esther Juliet (Juliet: "youthful")
- Hadassah Ruth

5.
QUEENS AND FIGURES OF COURT - JOSHUA TO ESTHER

An exploration of the women who navigated the complex worlds of monarchy, politics, and power in ancient Israel and its surrounding empires, from the period of the Judges through the Persian exile.

ACHSAH (עַכְסָה)

Pronunciation: AK-sah
Original Language: Hebrew
Core Meaning: "Anklet" or "Bangle" (from the tinkling sound of jewelry).

The Biblical Narrative: Achsah appears in the Book of Joshua (Joshua 15:16-19; Judges 1:12-15) not as a queen, but as a pivotal courtly figure—the daughter of Caleb, the faithful spy and Judahite prince. Her story is one of bold advocacy. Caleb promises her in marriage to the warrior who captures the city of Kiriath-sepher. His nephew, Othniel (who would later become Israel's first judge), succeeds. Upon her departure to her new home, Achsah does not remain passive. She "urged" or "persuaded" Othniel to ask her father for a field. Then, she herself takes direct action. Alighting from her donkey—a gesture of humility and respect—she approaches her father Caleb. When he asks, "What do you want?" she replies with stunning clarity: "Give me a blessing. Since you have given me the land of the Negeb, give me also springs of water." Caleb grants her request, giving her the upper and lower springs. Her story is brief but powerful: a woman who understood that land without water was an incomplete inheritance, and who possessed the courage and wit to secure her own future prosperity.

Cultural & Historical Context: In the patriarchal, clan-based society of early Israel during the Conquest and Settlement period (c. 1200-1000 BCE), women were legally dependent. Achsah's story provides a fascinating glimpse into the agency a woman of high status could exercise. As the daughter of a tribal leader, she had access and a voice. Her request for springs was not mere materialism; it was a claim to viable, sustainable economic power. Water rights were the ultimate source of life and wealth in the arid Negev. Her story reflects the tension between established social structures and the practical, often personal, negotiations that shaped daily life and legacy within leading Israelite families.

Modern Use & Legacy: Achsah is an exceptionally rare name in modern times, offering profound uniqueness. It carries a legacy of boldness, intelligence, and the pursuit of a secure foundation. It speaks to a parent's hope for a daughter who is both graceful (as the "anklet" implies) and assertively wise.

Middle-Name Pairing Suggestions:
Achsah Grace (highlighting the "blessing" she sought)
Achsah Noelle (combining ancient uniqueness with a modern, elegant flow)
Achsah Rivka (Rebekah; pairing with another biblically assertive woman)

Achsah Jade (a short, strong name complementing its distinctive sound)

JERIOTH (יְרִיעוֹת)

Pronunciation: yeh-ree-OHT or JER-ee-oth
Original Language: Hebrew
Core Meaning: "Curtains," "Tapestries," or "Tent Draperies."

The Biblical Narrative: Jerioth is mentioned in a single, genealogical verse in 1 Chronicles (1 Chron. 2:18). She is listed as a wife (or possibly a concubine) of Caleb ben Hezron, and the mother of his sons. The text states: "Caleb the son of Hezron had children by his wife Azubah, and by Jerioth..." Her placement in the lineage of the tribe of Judah, which leads to King David, is her sole claim to note. The Chronicler, writing post-exile, was intensely interested in establishing pure and legitimate lineages for the returning community. Jerioth's inclusion, even as a minor figure, signifies her importance in preserving that sacred line.

Cultural & Historical Context: During the period of the monarchy and later (the Chronicler wrote c. 400-250 BCE), genealogy was a primary source of identity, land rights, and social status. Women in these lists, often with only a name preserved, were vital links in the chain of descent. The meaning of her name, "Curtains," is intriguing. It may suggest a connection to beauty, craftsmanship, or the interior, domestic sphere of the court or wealthy household. It could also simply be an older name whose common meaning had faded. Her story is one of silent legacy—a reminder that history is built not only by those whose deeds are recorded, but by those whose bloodlines carried the promise forward.

Modern Use & Legacy: Virtually unused today, Jerioth is a deeply historical and obscure choice. It would appeal to parents with a love for archaeological or textual depth, symbolizing a connection to the hidden, foundational threads of history.

Middle-Name Pairing Suggestions:
Jerioth Elaine (softening the ancient with a classic)
Jerioth Beth (a simple, strong biblical anchor)
Jerioth Pearl (evoking the idea of a hidden gem in history)
Jerioth Selah (a poetic, reflective biblical word)

MAACHAH (מַעֲכָה)

Pronunciation: mah-ah-KAH
Original Language: Hebrew
Core Meaning: "Pressed," "Oppressed," or potentially "Burning."

The Biblical Narrative: Two significant royal women bear this name, creating a complex legacy.

1. Maacah, Daughter of Talmai, Wife of David (2 Sam. 3:3; 1 Chron. 3:2): She was a princess of the small Aramean kingdom of Geshur, married to David as a political alliance to secure his eastern border. She was the mother of Absalom, whose infamous rebellion was sparked by the rape of his sister Tamar and the murder of her brother Amnon. Through her, Absalom found refuge in her father's kingdom of Geshur after killing Amnon.

2. Maacah, Mother of King Asa (1 Kings 15:9-13; 2 Chron. 15:16): This Maacah (likely the grandmother, not mother, of Asa) held the powerful position of Gebirah —Queen Mother. She was a cultic leader who made an "abominable image" for the fertility goddess Asherah. King Asa, in his religious reforms, deposed her from her position and destroyed the idol. Her story illustrates the intense conflict between Canaanite fertility worship and the worship of Yahweh within the royal court itself.

Cultural & Historical Context: The Gebirah (Great Lady) was often the most powerful woman in the kingdom, wielding significant political and religious influence. Foreign princesses like David's wife Maacah were living peace treaties, but their presence also introduced foreign deities and customs. The struggle against idolatry in Judah was often a literal struggle within the palace walls, with the Queen Mother's household being a key battleground. Maacah's name, possibly meaning "oppressed," takes on ironic depth given her high status and eventual deposition.

Modern Use & Legacy: Maacah (sometimes Anglicized as Maacah or Maakah) is rare but usable. It carries a weight of political intrigue, maternal influence, and the tension between power and faith. It's a name for a story with shadows and substance.

Middle-Name Pairing Suggestions:
Maacah Tirzah (Tirzah was an early capital; a strong, regal pairing)
Maacah Hope (contrasting its potentially somber meaning)
Maacah Abigail (pairing with another politically astute biblical woman)
Maacah Ruth (balancing its complexity with a name of pure loyalty)

BATHSHEBA (בַּת־שֶׁבַע)

Pronunciation: bath-SHEE-bah or BATH-sheh-bah
Original Language: Hebrew
Core Meaning: "Daughter of the Oath" or "Daughter of Abundance/Seven."

The Biblical Narrative: Bathsheba's story is one of the Bible's most famous and fraught (2 Samuel 11-12; 1 Kings 1-2). Initially the wife of Uriah the Hittite, she is seen by King David from his rooftop, summoned, and an adulterous union takes place while her husband is at war. The resulting pregnancy leads David to orchestrate Uriah's death. After her mourning period, David marries her. The prophet Nathan confronts David, and the child dies. Bathsheba's later narrative shows a transformed woman of agency. She becomes the mother of Solomon. When David is old and another son, Adonijah, attempts to seize the throne, Bathsheba, prompted by the prophet Nathan, acts decisively. She approaches the king to remind him of his oath that Solomon would succeed him, securing her son's crown and her own position as Gebirah. She is listed in Matthew's genealogy of Jesus, a testament to God's grace working through deeply flawed history.

Cultural & Historical Context: Bathsheba's story exposes the absolute power of a Near Eastern monarch and the vulnerability of even elite citizens (Uriah was a trusted officer). Her later role is a textbook example of the Queen Mother's power as a royal advocate and kingmaker. Her transition from victim of royal abuse to a shrewd political actor at the heart of the succession struggle reveals the complex avenues of influence available to women in the royal household.

Modern Use & Legacy: Bathsheba is a classic, recognized biblical name with a rich, dramatic history. It has literary cachet (Hardy's Far From the Madding Crowd) and signifies beauty, resilience, and profound redemption. It's a bold choice, embracing a full spectrum of human experience.

Middle-Name Pairing Suggestions:
Bathsheba Grace (emphasizing the redemptive theme)
Bathsheba Anne (a classic, softening complement)
Bathsheba Noor (Arabic for "light," a beautiful intercultural pairing)
Bathsheba Jane (a straightforward, strong anchor)

ABISHAG (אֲבִישַׁג)

Pronunciation: AB-ih-shag
Original Language: Hebrew
Core Meaning: "My Father Strayed" or, more poetically, "Father of Error."

The Biblical Narrative: Abishag the Shunammite appears in the twilight of David's reign (1 Kings 1:1-4, 15; 2:13-25). A beautiful young woman from Shunem, she is brought to the aged, frail King David to "lie in his bosom" and warm him, though the text is careful to note "the king knew her not." After David's death, his son Adonijah, who had previously failed to seize the throne, requests Abishag as a wife from the new king, Solomon. Solomon interprets this not as a romantic request, but as a brazen political move to claim the former king's concubine—a symbolic act of claiming the throne itself. He orders Adonijah's execution. Abishag, a pawn in a deadly power struggle, disappears from the narrative.

Cultural & Historical Context: Abishag's role is a specific royal custom: a young, healthy companion for an infirm king, a role with both practical and symbolic significance. In the ancient world, access to the king's harem was synonymous with a claim to his authority (cf. Absalom's act in 2 Samuel 16:21-22). Solomon's violent reaction to Adonijah's request underscores this political reality. Abishag represents the tragic vulnerability of individuals, especially women, caught in the machinations of dynastic politics.

Modern Use & Legacy: Extremely rare, Abishag is a name of haunting beauty and tragic nobility. It appeals to those drawn to obscure biblical stories and names with a melancholic, poetic resonance.

Middle-Name Pairing Suggestions:
Abishag Rose (balancing its harsh meaning with floral softness)
Abishag Lily (similar effect, with purity connotations)
Abishag Shiloh (another peaceful, place-based biblical name)
Abishag Dove (symbolizing peace and innocence)

JEDIDAH (יְדִידָה)

Pronunciation: yeh-dee-DAH
Original Language: Hebrew
Core Meaning: "Beloved."

The Biblical Narrative: Jedidah is mentioned only once, in a single verse introducing the reign of her son, King Josiah (2 Kings 22:1). The text states: "Josiah was eight years old when he began to reign, and he reigned thirty-one years in Jerusalem. His mother's name was Jedidah the daughter of Adaiah of Bozkath." Her sole significance is her motherhood of one of Judah's most righteous and reforming kings, who rediscovered the Book of the Law and reinstated the Passover.

Cultural & Historical Context: As the mother of a child-king, Jedidah would have held immense influence as Gebirah during his minority. While the text does not detail her role, her name ("Beloved") and her son's profound piety suggest she was a positive, faithful influence in a court that had seen great idolatry under his grandfather, Manasseh. She represents the quiet, foundational influence of a godly mother in shaping a leader's character.

Modern Use & Legacy: Jedidah is a beautiful, melodic, and profoundly positive Hebrew name that remains underused. It is a direct synonym for "Amy" (from French aimée) or "Davina" (feminine of David, "beloved") but with deep biblical roots.

Middle-Name Pairing Suggestions:
Jedidah Ruth (a flowing, alliterative pairing of two virtuous names)
Jedidah Hope (reinforcing the positive meaning)
Jedidah Claire (a clear, bright classic complement)
Jedidah Tirzah (a uniquely biblical and regal combination)

HAMUTAL (חֲמוּטַל)

Pronunciation: hah-moo-TAHL
Original Language: Hebrew
Core Meaning: "Father-in-Law is Dew" or "Kinsman of Dew."
Dew was a powerful symbol of blessing and sustenance in
arid Israel.

The Biblical Narrative: Hamutal was a Queen of Judah, the
wife of King Josiah and mother of two of his successors, both
of whom had disastrous reigns (2 Kings 23:31; 24:18). She was
the mother of King Jehoahaz, who reigned three months
before being deposed by Pharaoh Neco, and King Zedekiah,
the last king of Judah, who witnessed the destruction of
Jerusalem and the Temple by Nebuchadnezzar. She is noted
as the daughter of Jeremiah of Libnah.

Cultural & Historical Context: Hamutal lived through the death
of her husband Josiah at Megiddo, the rapid decline of Judah
under Egyptian and Babylonian pressure, and the ultimate
catastrophe of the Exile. As the mother of the last king, she
likely endured the siege of Jerusalem and was almost
certainly taken into Babylonian captivity (2 Kings 24:15). Her
name, evoking life-giving dew, stands in stark, tragic contrast
to the barren destruction that marked her life and the end of
the Davidic monarchy.

Modern Use & Legacy: Hamutal is virtually unknown today
but is strikingly beautiful and sonorous. It is a name that
carries the weight of history's turning points, of tragedy and
resilience.

Middle-Name Pairing Suggestions:
Hamutal Grace (seeking grace amidst tragedy)
Hamutal Naomi (another biblical mother who knew deep loss)
Hamutal Shiloh (a name meaning "peace" or "tranquility")
Hamutal Rose (a symbol of beauty persisting among thorns)

6.
NAMES FROM THE POETIC BOOKS - JOB TO SONG OF SOLOMON

The poetic books of the Bible—Job, Psalms, and the Song of Songs—offer a distinct landscape for encountering women. Here, they appear not as actors in a historical narrative, but as subjects of profound reflection, as symbols of restored blessing, as voices of wisdom, and as the central figure in a sublime love poem. These names emerge from contexts of deep suffering, worshipful joy, and passionate intimacy, carrying meanings that resonate with the core human experiences of loss, hope, and love.

JEMIMAH (יְמִימָה – Yemimah)

Original Language & Core Meaning: Hebrew, יְמִימָה (Yemimah). The name is derived from yom (day), and most commonly understood to mean "dove." The dove is a universal symbol of peace, innocence, and renewal. Some scholars also connect it to the concept of "warmth" or "daylight," suggesting "fair as the day" or "little dove."

Biblical Narrative: Jemimah appears only once in Scripture, in the concluding chapter of Job (Job 42:14). She is the first of three daughters born to Job after the Lord restored his fortunes, following his unimaginable suffering and profound encounter with God. Her sisters are Keziah and Keren-Happuch. The text pointedly notes that Job gave these daughters an inheritance along with their brothers, an extraordinary act in the ancient world. Furthermore, it states that "in all the land there were no women so beautiful as the daughters of Job" (Job 42:15). Jemimah, whose name evokes purity and peace, stands as a living emblem of restoration. She is not a character with dialogue or action, but a symbol—the first fruit of Job's new life, a sign that the horror of loss has been transcended by a future of blessing and equity.

Cultural & Historical Context: In the patriarchal structure of the Ancient Near East, daughters were typically viewed in terms of their potential for marriage alliances. Their beauty was an asset, but their inheritance rights were severely limited. Job's actions—granting them an inheritance and singling out their unparalleled beauty—radically subvert these norms. It signals a blessing that transcends convention. The name itself, likely chosen by Job, reflects a conscious move away from the themes of grief (Bitter, No Incense, Not My People) that might have defined his earlier experience. Naming her "Dove" is an act of hope, reclaiming symbols of peace and God's favor (as in the dove returning to Noah's ark) after the storm.

Modern Use & Legacy: Jemimah is a rare and exquisite name in modern use. It carries a lyrical, vintage quality that appeals to parents seeking a truly distinctive biblical name with a powerfully positive story. Its association with beauty, peace, and restoration after trial gives it a deep, comforting resonance. It feels both classic and fresh, avoiding the trendiness of more common names.

Nicknames: Jem, Jemma, Mia, Mimi.
Middle Name Pairings: Jemimah Grace (emphasizing the gift), Jemimah Hope (focusing on the restoration), Jemimah Claire

(for clarity after suffering), Jemimah Ruth (pairing with another loyal beauty), Jemimah Elise.

KEZIAH (קְצִיעָה – Qetzi'ah)

Original Language & Core Meaning: Hebrew, קְצִיעָה (Qetzi'ah). The name means "cassia," a fragrant spice bark, closely related to cinnamon. Cassia was a precious ingredient in the sacred anointing oil used in the Tabernacle (Exodus 30:24). Thus, the name carries connotations of sacred fragrance, value, and consecration.

Biblical Narrative: Keziah is the second of Job's three restored daughters (Job 42:14). Like her sister Jemimah, she is a symbol of the abundant and precious blessing God bestowed upon Job in his latter days. Her name, meaning "cassia," elevates her from a mere symbol of restored family to a symbol of restored holiness and worth. The trials had, in a sense, anointed Job with suffering; his restoration includes daughters who bear the names of sacred perfumes, suggesting a life once again fragrant and pleasing, set apart for God.

Cultural & Historical Context: Spices like cassia were among the most valuable commodities of the ancient world, traded over vast distances from Arabia and India. They were used not only in worship but also in cosmetics, medicine, and as a display of extreme wealth. To name a daughter "Cassia" was to declare her preciousness. In the context of Job, a man known for his great wealth, naming a daughter after a luxury spice re-establishes his status, but with a sacred twist. It is no longer merely material wealth, but wealth imbued with a sense of divine favor and sacred purpose.

Modern Use & Legacy: Keziah is slightly more common than Jemimah but remains distinctive. It has a strong, zesty sound and a beautiful, exotic meaning. It appeals to parents drawn to nature names, spice names, or those seeking a biblical name with a tactile, sensory quality. Its connection to sacred anointing adds a layer of spiritual depth.

Nicknames: Kizzy, Kez, Zia, Kiah.
Middle Name Pairings: Keziah Faith (for sacred trust), Keziah Joy (for the fragrance of happiness), Keziah Noelle (combining precious gifts), Keziah Pearl (another precious natural element), Keziah Simone.

KEREN-HAPPUCH (קֶרֶן הַפּוּךְ – Qeren Happukh)

Original Language & Core Meaning: Hebrew, קֶרֶן הַפּוּךְ (Qeren Happukh). The name is a compound phrase meaning "horn of antimony" or "horn of eye-paint." Antimony was a black powder used as kohl, stored in a small horn container and applied to beautify and protect the eyes. The name thus signifies "container of beauty" or "radiance of beauty."

Biblical Narrative: Keren-Happuch is the third and youngest of Job's post-restoration daughters (Job 42:14). Her name completes a symbolic triad: Jemimah (innocent beauty/dove), Keziah (sacred fragrance), and Keren-Happuch (adorned, radiant beauty). This final name emphasizes not just natural beauty but cultivated and enhanced beauty—the art of adornment. It speaks to a restoration so complete that it includes not just life and holiness, but also joy, artistry, and the celebration of splendor.

Cultural & Historical Context: The use of kohl for the eyes was widespread in the ancient Near East and Egypt, worn by both men and women. It served practical purposes (reducing sun glare, protecting from infections) and profound aesthetic and symbolic ones, believed to ward off evil and enhance one's presence. A "horn" of this precious cosmetic was a valuable personal item. Naming a daughter after this object places her at the intersection of practicality, artistry, and value. It suggests a daughter who is both a practical vessel and a source of dazzling beauty.

Modern Use & Legacy: Keren-Happuch is almost never used in its full form today, given its length and unfamiliarity. However, "Keren" (קֶרֶן), meaning "horn" or "ray of light," is a common modern Hebrew name. In its full form, it is a bold, artistic, and historically rich choice for parents fascinated by biblical archaeology and the vividness of ancient life. It tells a story of resilience and the restoration of artistry.

Modern Adaptation: Keren or Karine.
Nicknames: (For Keren) Ren, Renny.
Middle Name Pairings (for Keren): Keren Bethany (house of beauty), Keren Elise, Keren Felicity (for happiness), Keren Lucille (light), Keren Daphne (laurel, victory).

THE SHULAMMITE (הַשּׁוּלַמִּית – HaShulammit)

Original Language & Core Meaning: Hebrew, הַשּׁוּלַמִּית (HaShulammit). This is not a personal name but a gentilic descriptor, meaning "the woman from Shulem" (likely Shunem). It may also be a feminine form of Shalom (peace), meaning "the peaceful one" or "the perfect one." She is the central female voice and figure in the Song of Songs.

Biblical Narrative: The Shulammite is the beloved in Solomon's passionate love poem. She is a rural woman from the vineyards, dark-skinned from working outdoors ("I am dark and lovely... because the sun has gazed upon me" – Song 1:5-6). The poem is a lyrical dialogue of mutual yearning, admiration, and pursuit between her and her lover (the king). She is assertive, articulate, and equal in passion. Her voice opens and closes the poem's narrative frame (Song 2:7, 3:5, 8:4), and she is the one who proclaims the central theme: "Love is as strong as death... its flames are a blazing fire" (Song 8:6). She represents ideal, passionate, and covenantal love.

Cultural & Historical Context: The Song of Songs stands apart in biblical literature for its unabashed celebration of erotic, mutual love within the covenant of marriage. The Shulammite, as a sun-darkened vineyard worker, challenges conventional ancient (and modern) standards of cloistered, pale feminine beauty. Her strength, her voice, and her active pursuit of her beloved present a uniquely powerful and egalitarian portrait of womanhood. The setting is pastoral and royal, blending images of nature (gardens, vineyards, flocks) with the luxury of the court, elevating human love to something both earthy and majestic.

Modern Use & Legacy: "Shulamith" (the common transliteration) is a recognized Hebrew name, though uncommon in English-speaking countries. It carries a tremendous weight of artistic, lyrical, and romantic association. It is a name for a child of profound depth, strength, and capacity for love. Its primary meaning of "peaceful" or "perfect" is beautiful, but its full context makes it a rich, complex choice.

Modern Form: Shulamith, Shula, Shulami.
Nicknames: Shuli, Shula, Lami.
Middle Name Pairings: Shulamith Rose (combining garden imagery), Shulamith Grace, Shulamith Joy, Shulamith Evangeline (good news of love), Shulamith Mara (bitter-sweet, acknowledging the "flames of jealousy" in love).

The women of the poetic books, though few in number, offer some of the most symbolically rich and emotionally resonant names in Scripture. They emerge from the ashes of suffering as signs of God's restorative beauty (Jemimah, Keziah, Keren-Happuch) and they stand at the heart of the Bible's great ode to human and divine love (The Shulammite). Their names invite us to consider our own stories of restoration and to embrace a vision of love that is strong, mutual, and filled with the fragrance of sacred commitment.

7.
NAMES FROM THE PROPHETIC BOOKS - ISAIAH TO MALACHI

This section explores the women mentioned in the prophetic books, moving from the pre-exilic warnings of Isaiah and Hosea to the exilic laments of Jeremiah and the post-exilic visions of Zechariah. These names are often deeply symbolic, serving as living metaphors for Israel's relationship with God. Their stories are less about individual biography and more about national destiny, making their names powerful, complex, and rich with theological meaning.

Hephzibah (חֶפְצִי־בָהּ)

Original Language & Core Meaning: Hebrew. "My delight is in her."

Biblical Narrative: Hephzibah appears not as an active character but as a symbolic name given to the restored city of Jerusalem, representing the future bride of God. In Isaiah 62:4, the prophet declares God's promise: "You shall no more be termed Forsaken, and your land shall no more be termed Desolate, but you shall be called Hephzibah, and your land

Beulah; for the LORD delights in you, and your land shall be married." This is a direct reversal of the judgment language used elsewhere. She is also historically the name of the wife of King Hezekiah and mother of the evil King Manasseh (2 Kings 21:1), though the prophetic use overshadows this.

Cultural & Historical Context: This prophecy was given during a time of deep national crisis, likely as Assyria threatened Judah. The name is a potent covenant reversal. Where Israel had been likened to an adulterous wife (Hosea), God now renames her as His beloved delight, echoing the intimate language of the Song of Solomon. It shifts identity from performance ("Forsaken" due to sin) to divine grace ("My delight").

Modern Use & Legacy: Rare but profoundly beautiful. It carries an aura of vintage elegance, deep theological significance, and a message of belovedness. It is a name for parents who cherish the promise of grace and restoration.

Middle-Name Pairing Suggestions: Hephzibah Grace, Hephzibah Joy, Hephzibah Rose, Hephzibah Maeve, Hephzibah Celeste.

Beulah (בְּעוּלָה)

Original Language & Core Meaning: Hebrew. "Married" or "Owned (as a wife)."

Biblical Narrative: Beulah is the companion promise to Hephzibah in Isaiah 62:4. The land itself, personified as a woman, will no longer be "Desolate" but "Beulah." This signifies the end of exile and spiritual barrenness, and the restoration of a full, covenant marriage relationship with Yahweh. It is the ultimate promise of homecoming and intimate union.

Cultural & Historical Context: In ancient Near Eastern law and covenant language, to be a wife was to have a status of protection, provision, and intimate belonging. For a land devastated by war and exile, the promise of being "married" again meant security, fertility (both agricultural and spiritual), and restored honor. It directly countered the trauma of being "forsaken."

Modern Use & Legacy: Used occasionally since the Puritan era, it has a soft, literary, and slightly antique feel. It symbolizes commitment, fruitfulness, and a heart for home. It is more approachable than Hephzibah but carries similar theological weight.

Middle-Name Pairing Suggestions: Beulah Anne, Beulah Faith, Beulah Hope, Beulah Claire, Beulah Josephine.

Ariel (אֲרִיאֵל)

Original Language & Core Meaning: Hebrew. "Lion of God" or "Hearth of God."

Biblical Narrative: In Isaiah 29, the prophet delivers a stern "woe" to Ariel, a symbolic name for Jerusalem (the city where David dwelt). God declares He will besiege Ariel and bring her low with mourning and lamentation. The name here is ironic; the "Lion of God" or "Altar Hearth" (the place of holy fire) will become a place of God's consuming judgment before a future, promised whisper of restoration (Isaiah 29:17-24).

Cultural & Historical Context: As Jerusalem, Ariel was the political and religious heart of Judah. Calling it "God's lion" may reference its intended strength and royal Davidic legacy. Calling it "God's hearth" points to the Temple altar. The prophecy warned that this sacred center was not immune to judgment for covenant faithlessness. It was a shocking concept to a people who believed Zion was inviolable.

Modern Use & Legacy: Primarily used as a male name (e.g., Shakespeare's spirit in The Tempest), but its "-el" ending (meaning "God") and literary pedigree have led to growing use for girls. For a daughter, it suggests divinely given strength, courage, and a fiery spirit.

Middle-Name Pairing Suggestions: Ariel Simone, Ariel Noelle, Ariel Juno, Ariel Beatrice, Ariel Skye.

The Daughter of Zion / The Virgin Daughter of Zion

Original Language & Core Meaning: Hebrew: Bat Tziyon (בַּת צִיּוֹן). "Daughter of Zion." A personification.

Biblical Narrative: This is the most pervasive female symbol in the prophets. From Isaiah to Micah to Zephaniah, "the Daughter of Zion" or "Virgin Daughter of Zion/Judah" is the collective personification of God's people. She is portrayed variously as a devastated widow (Lamentations), a rebellious child, a besieged princess, and, ultimately, a restored queen. God addresses the nation through this intimate, familial metaphor, expressing both fierce anger over her adultery with foreign gods and profound grief and compassion for her suffering (e.g., Isaiah 1:8, Lamentations 2).

Cultural & Historical Context: The metaphor draws on familial and royal imagery. As a "daughter," she is under God's protection and authority. As a "virgin" princess, she was set apart, betrothed to Yahweh. Her "adultery" is idolatry. Her devastation at the hands of Babylon is depicted as rape and slaughter. This personification made the national catastrophe unbearably personal and emotional.

Modern Use & Legacy: "Zion" itself is a powerful modern name for both boys and girls, carrying connotations of a spiritual utopia or homeland. While "Daughter of Zion" is not used as a given name, understanding this symbol is key to interpreting names like Zion, Tzipporah (related to "bird," but shares the 'Tzi' root), or Tziyona (a modern Hebrew feminine form).

Middle-Name Pairing Suggestions for Zion: Zion Mira, Zion Eliana, Zion Amara, Zion Ruth, Zion Dove.

Gomer (גֹּמֶר)

Original Language & Core Meaning: Hebrew. Likely "complete" or possibly related to a verb for "to come to an end."

Biblical Narrative: God commands the prophet Hosea to enact a living parable by marrying Gomer, "a wife of whoredom" (Hosea 1:2-3). She bears him children with symbolic names (Jezreel, Lo-Ruhamah, Lo-Ammi) and then is unfaithful, leaving him for other lovers. Hosea is commanded to buy her back from slavery (Hosea 3), mirroring God's relentless, redeeming love for idolatrous Israel. Gomer is less a developed character and more the central, tragic symbol of covenant unfaithfulness.

Cultural & Historical Context: Hosea's prophecy occurred in the Northern Kingdom of Israel just before its fall to Assyria (722 BC). Israel's widespread idolatry (especially Baal worship) is portrayed as spiritual prostitution. Gomer's story would have been scandalous and visceral, driving home the shame and pain Israel's behavior caused Yahweh, yet also showcasing a love that chooses to redeem the utterly unworthy.

Modern Use & Legacy: Extremely rare due to its direct association with prostitution. It is primarily known from the biblical story and has not seen positive adoption. It serves as a profound theological lesson rather than a viable name choice.

Middle-Name Pairing Suggestions: Not generally recommended for use.

Lo-Ruhamah (לֹא רֻחָמָה)

Original Language & Core Meaning: Hebrew. "Not loved," "Not pitied," or "She who has not received mercy."

Biblical Narrative: The second child born to Hosea and Gomer, a daughter. God instructs Hosea to name her Lo-Ruhamah, declaring, "for I will no more have mercy on the house of Israel, to forgive them at all" (Hosea 1:6). Her name is a shocking pronouncement of imminent, deserved judgment. Yet, in Hosea 2:23, the promise is reversed for Judah: "And I will have mercy on Lo-Ruhamah."

Cultural & Historical Context: In a culture where names were blessings, this name was a public curse and a prophetic sign. It announced the end of God's patience with the Northern Kingdom's entrenched sin. The withholding of rachamim (womb-like, tender mercies) signified a severing of the maternal bond of covenant care.

Modern Use & Legacy: Virtually unused as a given name for obvious reasons. However, the name Ruhamah (without the "Lo") exists as a very rare but beautiful choice, meaning "loved," "pitied," or "one who has received mercy."

Middle-Name Pairing Suggestions for Ruhamah: Ruhamah Grace, Ruhamah Hope, Ruhamah Dawn, Ruhamah Felicity, Ruhamah Eve.

The women of the prophets inhabit a world of metaphor and stark divine poetry. They are not individuals we follow through a life story, but powerful symbols—the beloved bride turned adulteress, the forsaken wife renamed in delight, the judged city, the unforgiven daughter. Their names (Hephzibah, Beulah) become promises etched onto a future hope. Others (Lo-Ruhamah, Gomer) are stark, painful signs of a broken covenant. To engage with these names is to engage with the deepest dynamics of sin and grace, judgment and restoration. They remind us that identity—whether personal or corporate—is ultimately defined by God's pronouncement. He names us according to our reality, yet in His redemptive love, He holds the power to rename us according to His grace.

8.
NAMES FROM THE FAMILY OF JESUS

Introduction to the Family Circle

In the Gospel narratives, the family of Jesus provides a complex, human backdrop to the divine story. While much attention focuses on Jesus Himself, the women in His family circle emerge from the text as pivotal witnesses, early followers, and bearers of a unique, often painful, legacy. They are not merely supporting characters; they are the first cradle of the Incarnation and, later, the nucleus of the early Church in Jerusalem. Their names—rooted in Hebrew tradition, yet echoing through Greek and Aramaic—carry the weight of Israel's past and the seismic shift of the New Covenant. To explore these names is to touch the intimate, relational heart of the Gospel story, where divine purpose intersected with an ordinary, yet extraordinary, family in Nazareth and beyond.

Mary (Μαριάμ / Μαρία) – Mother of Jesus

Original Language & Core Meaning: Hebrew/Aramaic: מִרְיָם (Miryam). The etymology is debated, with leading theories suggesting "bitterness" (from mar, bitter), "rebellion," or "wished-for child." In an Egyptian context, it could relate to mry ("beloved"). In the biblical tradition, its most famous bearer is Miriam, the sister of Moses—a prophetess and leader.

Greek: Μαριάμ (Mariam) or Μαρία (Maria). The New Testament uses both forms interchangeably.

Biblical Narrative: Mary's story is the cornerstone of the Nativity. A young virgin betrothed to Joseph in Nazareth, she is visited by the angel Gabriel, who announces she will conceive by the Holy Spirit and bear the Son of God (Luke 1:26-38). Her response, "Let it be to me according to your word," is the pinnacle of faithful surrender. She visits her relative Elizabeth, proclaiming the Magnificat (Luke 1:46-55). She gives birth in Bethlehem, treasures the shepherds' words, and presents Jesus in the Temple (Luke 2). She and Joseph flee to Egypt, return to Nazareth, and are seen anxiously searching for the 12-year-old Jesus in Jerusalem (Luke 2:41-51). At the wedding in Cana, she prompts Jesus' first public sign, receiving a gentle rebuke that signals a shift in their relationship (John 2:1-5). She is present at the cross, where Jesus entrusts her to the care of the Beloved Disciple (John 19:25-27). Finally, she is listed among the believers praying in the upper room after the Ascension (Acts 1:14).

Cultural & Historical Context: Mary was a Jewish peasant girl in a small village in Galilee, a region often looked down upon by the Judean elite. Her betrothal (a legally binding first stage of marriage) and subsequent pregnancy outside of full cohabitation placed her in a socially perilous position, requiring divine intervention through Joseph. Her song, the Magnificat, echoes the songs of Hannah and other Old Testament women, rooting the revolutionary news of the Gospel—the humbling of the proud and exaltation of the lowly—in the tradition of Jewish faith. As Jesus' ministry began, her role transitioned from mother to follower, a painful but necessary journey of faith.

Spiritual Legacy: Mary embodies kenosis (self-emptying) and obedient faith. She is the Theotokos (God-bearer), the human vessel for the Incarnation. Her life is a testament to God's favor resting on the humble, her heart "pierced" as Simeon prophesied (Luke 2:35), and her faithfulness extends from the manger to the cross to the birth of the Church.

Modern Use & Middle-Name Pairings: Mary remains a timeless classic, perpetually in use across Christian cultures. Its simplicity and profound heritage give it enduring strength.

Classic Pairings: Mary Catherine, Mary Elizabeth, Mary Margaret, Mary Josephine.
Floral/Simple Pairings: Mary Rose, Mary Grace, Mary Claire, Mary Jane.
Modern/Versatile Pairings: Mary Sophia, Mary Elise, Mary Beatrice, Mary Fiona.

Elizabeth (Ἐλισάβετ)

Original Language & Core Meaning: Hebrew: אֱלִישֶׁבַע (Elisheva), meaning "My God is an oath" or "God is my abundance." Greek: Ἐλισάβετ (Elisabet).

Biblical Narrative: Elizabeth, a descendant of Aaron, is married to the priest Zechariah. Both are described as "righteous before God" but childless and advanced in years (Luke 1:5-7). While Zechariah is serving in the Temple, the angel Gabriel appears to him, announcing that Elizabeth will bear a son to be named John. Zechariah questions this and is rendered mute. Elizabeth conceives and goes into seclusion. Six months into her pregnancy, she is visited by her relative Mary. Upon Mary's greeting, Elizabeth's unborn child (John the Baptist) leaps in her womb, she is filled with the Holy Spirit, and she proclaims a blessing over Mary and the child she carries (Luke 1:39-45). She later gives birth to John, and at his circumcision, she confirms his name, defying family tradition (Luke 1:57-60).

Cultural & Historical Context: In a culture that saw childlessness as a potential sign of divine disfavor, Elizabeth's barrenness was a deep sorrow and social shame. As a priest's wife, the pressure would have been acute. Her pregnancy in old age mirrors the pattern of Sarah, Rebekah, and Hannah, signaling a special work of God. Her prophetic utterance upon Mary's arrival breaks the silence imposed on her husband and positions her as the first person to verbally recognize the Messiah, even in utero.

Spiritual Legacy: Elizabeth represents God's faithfulness to His covenant and His power to bring life from barrenness. She is a model of patient, righteous living rewarded. Her Spirit-filled recognition of Jesus underscores that divine revelation transcends age, gender, and social expectation.

Modern Use & Middle-Name Pairings: Elizabeth is a regal, enduring name with a wealth of nickname options (Eliza, Liz, Beth, Ellie, Elise). It carries a sense of intelligence, grace, and strength.

Traditional Pairings: Elizabeth Anne, Elizabeth Grace, Elizabeth Mary, Elizabeth Victoria.
Contemporary Pairings: Elizabeth Wren, Elizabeth Sage, Elizabeth Noelle, Elizabeth Joy.

Nickname-Focused: Eliza June, Bethany Rose, Elle Margaret, Liza Claire.

Mary, the wife of Clopas

Original Language & Core Meaning: See Mary above.

Biblical Narrative: She appears only once, in John's Gospel, standing near the cross of Jesus: "But standing by the cross of Jesus were his mother and his mother's sister, Mary the wife of Clopas, and Mary Magdalene" (John 19:25). The phrasing is ambiguous—she is either the sister of Jesus' mother (which would mean two sisters named Mary, unlikely but possible) or, more probably, a sister-in-law or close relative referred to as a "sister." She is often identified with "Mary the mother of James the younger and of Joseph" mentioned in the Synoptic Gospels (Matthew 27:56; Mark 15:40), who witnesses the crucifixion, the burial, and goes to the tomb on Easter morning.

Cultural & Historical Context: Her identification as the wife of Clopas (likely the Greek form of the Aramaic Alphaeus) links her to the wider family and apostolic circle. Clopas/Alphaeus is traditionally understood as the father of the apostle James the Less. Her presence at the cross, a scene of utmost danger and despair, highlights remarkable courage and loyalty. She was part of the Galilean women who followed Jesus to Jerusalem, supporting the ministry financially and personally (Luke 8:1-3).

Spiritual Legacy: She embodies the faithful, often overlooked, supporter. Her legacy is one of steadfast presence in the darkest hour and witness to the key events of redemption. She represents the many unnamed disciples whose quiet faithfulness forms the backbone of the Christian community.

Modern Use & Middle-Name Pairings: As a Mary, the same principles apply. However, using "Mary Clopas" or "Mary of Clopas" would be an extraordinarily specific and learned choice. For a more subtle tribute, pairing Mary with a name meaning "steadfast" or "brave" could honor her character.

Virtue-Based Pairings: Mary Constance, Mary Verity, Mary Felicity.
Simple & Strong: Mary Kate, Mary Joan, Mary Louise.

Salome

Original Language & Core Meaning: Hebrew: שְׁלוֹמִית (Shlomit), the feminine form of שָׁלוֹם (Shalom), meaning "peace." Greek: Σαλώμη (Salōmē).

Biblical Narrative: Salome is not explicitly named in the Synoptic crucifixion accounts but is reliably identified by early tradition and textual deduction. Mark 15:40 lists the women at the cross as "Mary Magdalene, and Mary the mother of James the younger and of Joses, and Salome." This Salome is then identified in Mark 16:1 as one of the women who brought spices to the tomb. She is also often identified as the mother of the sons of Zebedee (James and John), who asked Jesus for positions of honor for her sons (Matthew 20:20-21). If this identification is correct, she was also present with the other women at the crucifixion and empty tomb.

Cultural & Historical Context: As the mother of two prominent apostles and a follower of Jesus herself, Salome was likely a woman of some means, part of the group supporting Jesus' ministry. Her request for her sons' precedence, while ambitious, shows a mother's devotion and a misunderstanding of Jesus' servant-hearted kingdom. Her presence at the cross and tomb demonstrates that this ambition was refined into faithful, courageous discipleship.

Spiritual Legacy: Salome's story is one of transformation—from a mother seeking worldly status for her children to a disciple witnessing the cost and victory of the cross. She represents the journey of learning that God's peace (shalom) is found not in exaltation, but in faithful service and witness.

Modern Use & Middle-Name Pairings: Salome is a distinctive, beautiful name with a strong historical and artistic aura (associated with the dancer in the Gospel of Mark 6). It is more common in European languages than in English but is gaining attention for its melodic sound and peaceful meaning.

Elegant Pairings: Salome Eleanor, Salome Iris, Salome Beatrice, Salome Vivienne.

Simple & Sweet: Salome Grace, Salome Ruth, Salome Jane, Salome Claire.
Cultural Fusion: Salome Noor, Salome Lucia, Salome Fleur.

These women—Mary, Elizabeth, Mary of Clopas, and Salome—formed the essential, human first community of faith around Jesus. They were His first home, His early supporters, His faithful witnesses at His death, and the first recipients and proclaimers of the news of His resurrection. Their names, echoing the hopes of Israel (Miriam, Elisheva, Shlomit), were fulfilled in ways they could not have imagined. Choosing a name from this intimate circle connects a child not only to a individual story of faith, courage, or devotion but also to the very heart of the Christian story: a family who loved, followed, and bore witness to the Savior of the world.

9.
NAMES OF WOMEN TRANSFORMED BY CHRIST

A Necessary Prelude: The Challenge of Chronology

Before we walk this sacred ground, we must acknowledge a difficulty. The Gospels are not modern biographies with precise timelines. Matthew, Mark, Luke, and John arrange their accounts thematically, theologically, and sometimes geographically rather than chronologically. The Acts of the Apostles, our only canonical record of the early church, follows a roughly linear progression but often condenses years into paragraphs.

Therefore, the "chronological order" presented here is a careful construction—harmonizing the four Gospel accounts with scholarly consensus regarding the likely sequence of Jesus's ministry, while recognizing that absolute certainty remains elusive. The women themselves, in many cases unnamed in the text, have been preserved for us not by date-stamps but by the indelible mark of their encounters with Christ. Their chronological arrangement is offered not as dogmatic assertion but as devotional framework, allowing us to trace the expanding ripples of transformation from Galilee to Jerusalem to the ends of the earth.

Simon's Mother-in-Law
The First Recorded Healing of a Woman by Jesus

Original Language & Core Meaning: Her name is not recorded. In Greek, she is identified only as ἡ πενθερὰ Σίμωνος (hē penthera Simōnos)—"the mother-in-law of Simon." The absence of her name is itself a historical reality of first-century patriarchal recording, yet her anonymity has not diminished her significance.

The Biblical Narrative: Her story appears in Matthew 8:14–15, Mark 1:29–31, and Luke 4:38–39. The scene unfolds immediately following Jesus's first public teaching in Capernaum. He enters the home of Simon (Peter) and Andrew. The woman lies ill with a severe fever—Luke, the physician, uses the medical term πυρετὸς μέγας (pyretos megas), "a great fever."

What happens next is extraordinary in its tenderness and its abruptness. Jesus does not demand faith declared aloud. He does not require her to rise and come to him. He approaches her bed. He takes her hand. The fever departs. And then— this is the mark of genuine transformation—she rises and begins to serve them. The Greek word used is διηκόνει (diēkonei), the same root from which we derive "deacon." Her healing becomes her commissioning.

Cultural & Historical Context: A first-century Jewish woman's domain was the home, yet even within that sphere, illness rendered her unable to fulfill her household responsibilities. Her fever was not merely physical distress; it was social dislocation. By healing her, Jesus restored not only her body but her place in her community. The text's matter-of-fact inclusion of Peter's marital status also quietly affirms that celibacy was not required for apostolic calling.

Modern Use & Middle-Name Pairings: While the mother-in-law herself is unnamed, her legacy invites reflection on the countless unnamed women whose service undergirded the early church. For parents drawn to her story, consider:
- Simonetta ("little Simon") paired with Grace —honoring the household of Simon Peter while celebrating the unearned favor of healing.

Tabitha paired with Ruth —linking two servant-hearted women whose transformed lives produced tangible works of compassion.

The Samaritan Woman at Jacob's Well
Photini, the Equal-to-the-Apostles

Original Language & Core Meaning: The Gospel of John identifies her only as γυνὴ ἐκ τῆς Σαμαρείας (gynē ek tēs Samareias)—"a woman from Samaria." Eastern Orthodox tradition names her Photini (Φωτεινή), meaning "enlightened one" or "the luminous." The name derives from φῶς (phōs), "light." It is a post-resurrection name, given not at birth but in recognition of her transformed identity.

The Biblical Narrative: John 4:4–42 preserves the longest recorded conversation between Jesus and any individual in the Gospels. The woman comes to Jacob's well at the sixth hour—noon—an unusual time for water-drawing, suggesting she avoided the communal evening gathering. Jesus, breaching three cultural barriers simultaneously (gender, ethnicity, moral reputation), asks her for a drink.

Their dialogue moves from literal water to living water, from physical thirst to spiritual satisfaction. Jesus reveals his knowledge of her five previous husbands and her current, unmarriage relationship. She does not flee or deny. She names the Messiah question that divided Jews and Samaritans. And Jesus, to her alone before his trial, explicitly declares: Ἐγώ εἰμι, ὁ λαλῶν σοι (Egō eimi, ho lalōn soi)—"I am he, the one speaking to you."

She leaves her water jar—the very purpose of her journey—and becomes the first evangelist to the Samaritans. Many believe because of her testimony. Her transformation is complete: from shamed outcast to apostolic witness.

Cultural & Historical Context: Samaritans were despised by Jews as ethnic and religious half-breeds, their worship at Mount Gerizim deemed illegitimate. A Jewish man speaking publicly to a Samaritan woman was scandalous; her moral reputation compounded the breach. That Jesus entrusts her with the first explicit "I am" declaration in John's Gospel signals the radical inversion of his kingdom: the last shall be first, and the shamed shall be the herald.

Modern Use & Middle-Name Pairings:

Photini —rare in the West, treasured in the East; a name for a daughter destined to carry light into dark places.

Photini Grace —light and unearned favor

Photini Faith —the believing heart that proclaims

Samara —derived from Samaria; a more accessible contemporary option.

Samara Joy —the well of living water becomes a source of gladness

Samara Hope —the woman who hoped in the coming Messiah and found him standing before her

---

The Woman with the Issue of Blood
Haemorrhoissa, the Daughter of Faith

Original Language & Core Meaning: Tradition names her variously; the Greek text calls her simply γυνὴ (gynē)—"a woman." In Eastern Christian tradition, she is Veronica (from vera icona, "true image"), though this association developed later. The medical condition described, αἱμορροοῦσα (haimorroousa), denotes chronic hemorrhaging.

The Biblical Narrative: Matthew 9:20–22, Mark 5:25–34, and Luke 8:43–48 preserve her story with vivid, almost cinematic detail. Twelve years she has suffered. She has spent all her living on physicians who only made her worse. She is, by Levitical law, perpetually unclean—unable to participate in worship, unable to touch or be touched, a living exile in her own community.

She moves through the crowd. She thinks, Ἐὰν ἅψωμαι κἂν τῶν ἱματίων αὐτοῦ (Ean hapsōmai kan tōn himatiōn autou) —"If I touch even his garments." Her touch is ritual defilement; his garment's fringe (tzitzit) bears the command of Numbers 15. She touches. The fountain of blood dries.

Jesus stops. Τίς μου ἥψατο; (Tis mou hēpsato?)—"Who touched me?" The disciples protest the impossibility of the question. But Jesus knows power has gone out from him. The woman, fearing and trembling, falls before him and tells the whole truth. And Jesus speaks the word that transforms her condition into her identity: Θυγάτηρ (Thygatēr). "Daughter."

Twelve years of uncleanness. One touch of faith. And she is no longer defined by her hemorrhage but by her adoption.

Cultural & Historical Context: Her twelve years of suffering parallel the twelve-year-old daughter of Jairus, whom Jesus raises immediately following this encounter—Mark intentionally intercalates the two stories. Chronic bleeding rendered her not only physically depleted but ceremonially untouchable. Her act of touching Jesus was an act of profound desperation and audacious faith, violating purity codes in hope of healing. Jesus's response—praising her faith, calling her "daughter"—restores not only her body but her place in the covenant community.

Modern Use & Middle-Name Pairings:
Veronica —the Western traditional name, bearing the echo of her courageous approach.

Veronica Faith —she touched in faith and was made whole

Veronica Joy —from suffering to rejoicing

Bernice —from Pherenike, "bearer of victory"; a Hellenistic Jewish name found elsewhere in the New Testament.

Bernice Hope —the hope that dared to reach

Jairus's Daughter
Talitha, the Child Awakened

Original Language & Core Meaning: Mark 5:41 preserves the very Aramaic words of Jesus: Ταλιθὰ κούμ (Talitha koum). Talitha (טליתא) means "little girl" or "lamb"; koum (קומי) means "arise." It is the only instance in the Gospels where Jesus's exact Aramaic speech to a woman or girl is recorded. Matthew 9:18–26 and Luke 8:40–56 also recount her raising.

The Biblical Narrative: Jairus, a synagogue ruler, falls at Jesus's feet, begging him to heal his twelve-year-old daughter. As Jesus travels, the woman with the hemorrhage intercepts him. Then messengers arrive: Ἡ θυγάτηρ σου ἀπέθανεν (Hē thygatēr sou apethanen)—"Your daughter has died." Jesus speaks: Μὴ φοβοῦ, μόνον πίστευσον (Mē phobou, monon pisteuson)—"Do not fear, only believe."

At the house, professional mourners have already assembled. Jesus insists she is not dead but sleeping. They laugh at him. He takes the child's hand and speaks the Aramaic words her own mother might have used to rouse her from sleep: Talitha koum. Her spirit returns. She rises. She walks. And Jesus, remarkably, tells them to give her something to eat.

Cultural & Historical Context: A twelve-year-old girl in first-century Judaism stood at the threshold of womanhood, likely betrothed or nearing betrothal. Her death was not merely the loss of a child but the extinguishing of a family's future lineage. Jesus's instruction to feed her is profoundly human and theologically significant: the resurrection is not ghostly apparition but embodied, continued life. She is not a spirit; she is a hungry girl.

Modern Use & Middle-Name Pairings:

Talitha —a direct inheritance of Jesus's own tender address.
Talitha Grace —the little lamb raised by divine favor
Talitha Joy —mourning turned to dancing
Jairus —though masculine in form, occasionally used for girls; the father whose desperate faith brought Jesus to his daughter's bedside. Or possibly, Jairia, a more feminine version.
Ariel —"lion of God"; a Hebrew name evoking strength, paired with Talitha for the lamb who was raised.

The Canaanite (Syrophoenician) Woman
The Mother Who Argued with God

Original Language & Core Meaning: Matthew 15:22 calls her
*γυνὴ Χαναναία (gynē Chananaia)—"a Canaanite woman."
Mark 7:26 refines the designation: Ἑλληνίς, Συροφοινίκισσα
τῷ γένει (Hellēnis, Syrophoinikissa tō genei)—"a Greek, a
Syrophoenician by birth." Her name is unrecorded; her
identity is preserved through her ethnicity and her desperate
plea.

The Biblical Narrative: This is perhaps the most startling
encounter in the Gospels. A Gentile woman whose region is
pagan, whose people historically oppressed Israel, cries out:
Ἐλέησόν με, Κύριε, υἱὸς Δαυίδ (Eleēson me, Kyrie, huios
Dauid)—"Have mercy on me, Lord, Son of David." Jesus does
not answer. The disciples urge him to send her away. He
responds: Οὐκ ἀπεστάλην εἰ μὴ εἰς τὰ πρόβατα τὰ
ἀπολωλότα οἴκου Ἰσραήλ (Ouk apestalēn ei mē eis ta
probata ta apolōlota oikou Israēl)—"I was sent only to the lost
sheep of the house of Israel."

She kneels. She worships. She pleads: Κύριε, βοήθει μοι
(Kyrie, boēthei moi)—"Lord, help me."

And Jesus speaks words that have troubled readers for two
millennia: Οὐκ ἔστιν καλὸν λαβεῖν τὸν ἄρτον τῶν τέκνων καὶ
βαλεῖν τοῖς κυναρίοις (Ouk estin kalon labein ton arton tōn
teknōn kai balein tois kynariois)—"It is not right to take the
children's bread and throw it to the little dogs."

The Greek word is diminutive: κυναρίοις (kynariois), "little
dogs," house pets rather than the wild scavengers of the
streets. But the sting remains. And she does not retreat. She
takes his metaphor and turns it back upon him with the
audacity of a mother who will not be refused:

Καί, Κύριε· καὶ γὰρ τὰ κυνάρια ἐσθίει ἀπὸ τῶν ψιχίων τῶν πιπτόντων ἀπὸ τῆς τραπέζης τῶν κυρίων αὐτῶν (Kai, Kyrie; kai gar ta kynaria esthiei apo tōn psichiōn tōn piptontōn apo tēs trapezēs tōn kyriōn autōn)—"Yes, Lord; yet even the little dogs eat the crumbs that fall from their masters' table."

Jesus responds with astonishment: ˚Ω γύναι, μεγάλη σου ἡ πίστις (Ō gynai, megalē sou hē pistis)—"O woman, great is your faith!" Her daughter is healed that very hour.

Cultural & Historical Context: The epithet "Canaanite" deliberately evokes Israel's ancient enemies, the inhabitants of the promised land whom the Israelites were commanded to dispossess. That a woman from this lineage calls Jesus "Son of David" is theologically explosive. Her persistence, her willingness to engage in theological debate, her acceptance of the metaphor and her creative reframing of it—all of this occurs outside the boundaries of Israel, on Gentile soil, and becomes the occasion for Jesus's praise of "great faith" surpassing anything he has found in Israel.

Modern Use & Middle-Name Pairings:
Syra —from Syrophoenician; a short, strong contemporary name.
Syra Faith —great faith from unexpected places
Syra Hope —the crumbs that become a feast
Phoenicia —the full geographical designation; uncommon and distinctive.
Cana —evoking both her Canaanite identity and the wedding at Cana where Jesus's mother interceded.
Cana Grace —crumbs and wedding wine, both abundance from perceived scarcity

---

Mary Magdalene
The Tower, The Apostle to the Apostles

Original Language & Core Meaning: Μαρία ἡ Μαγδαληνή (*Maria hē Magdalēnē*). Maria is the Greek form of Miryam (מרים), whose meaning is debated: "bitterness," "beloved," "rebellion," or "wished-for child." Magdalēnē denotes her origin: Magdala, a fishing village on the western shore of the Sea of Galilee, whose name derives from migdal (מגדל), meaning "tower."

The Biblical Narrative: Luke 8:1–3 introduces her in a catalogue of women who accompanied Jesus and the Twelve, "and also some women who had been cured of evil spirits and diseases: Mary (called Magdalene), from whom seven demons had come out." Seven is the number of completion; her deliverance was total, her transformation complete. She becomes one of the women who "were helping to support them out of their own means"—financial patrons of the itinerant ministry.

She stands at the cross when the disciples have fled. Mark 15:40 lists her among the women watching from a distance. Matthew 27:56 places her there. John 19:25 records her presence at the crucifixion itself. She observes where Joseph of Arimathea lays Jesus's body. She returns at dawn on the first day of the week.

And to her, first, the risen Christ appears.

John 20:11–18 preserves the most intimate resurrection encounter. She weeps at the empty tomb. She sees two angels. She turns and sees Jesus, but does not recognize him. She mistakes him for the gardener. He speaks one word: Μαριάμ (Mariam). Her name. The shepherd's call. She answers: Ῥαββουνί (Rabbouni)—"My Teacher."

The apostolic commission is given not to Peter, not to John, but to her: Πορεύου δὲ πρὸς τοὺς ἀδελφούς μου καὶ εἰπὲ αὐτοῖς (Poreuou de pros tous adelphous mou kai epe autois) —"Go to my brothers and tell them." She becomes apostola apostolorum, the apostle to the apostles.

Cultural & Historical Context: Magdala was a prosperous fishing and fish-processing center. A woman identified by her hometown rather than by a husband's or father's name suggests either widowhood, singleness, or unusual economic independence. Her provision "out of her own means" indicates financial resources—perhaps inherited wealth or successful enterprise. The tradition conflating her with the sinful woman of Luke 7 has no biblical basis and was definitively rejected by the Catholic Church in 1969; the Eastern Church has always maintained the distinction. She is not a repentant prostitute. She is a delivered woman of means and means, faithful to the end and rewarded with the first sight of the risen Lord.

Modern Use & Middle-Name Pairings:
Mary —the English form; timeless, classic, weighted with two thousand years of devotion.
Mary Magdalene —the full name, reclaiming her from misidentification
Mary Grace —the unmerited favor of complete deliverance
Magdalena —the fuller form; popular in Eastern Europe and Latin America.
Magdalena Hope —the resurrection hope she first proclaimed
Magdalena Faith —the faith that waited at the tomb
Mara —from the root meaning "bitterness"; the name Naomi took in her grief (Ruth 1:20), transformed by the joy of resurrection.
Tower —as a virtue name; rare but evocative.
 Tower Grace —she was a tower of strength, raised by grace

Joanna
The Steward's Wife, The Resurrection Witness

Original Language & Core Meaning: Ἰωάννα (Iōanna), the feminine form of Ἰωάννης (Iōannēs, John), meaning "Yahweh has been gracious." Her name itself is a testimony of grace.

The Biblical Narrative: Luke 8:3 identifies her as "the wife of Chuza, Herod's steward." Herod Antipas, tetrarch of Galilee, maintained a substantial household; his steward (ἐπίτροπος, epitropos) was a position of significant responsibility, managing estates and finances. Joanna moved in circles of considerable political and economic power—and left them to follow an itinerant Galilean teacher.

She is listed among the women who provided for Jesus and the Twelve "out of their own means." Her resources, derived from her husband's position, were redirected to support the kingdom. Her presence in Jesus's entourage, given her connection to Herod's court, is remarkable and perhaps accounts for some of Luke's unique material regarding Herod's interest in Jesus (Luke 9:7–9; 23:6–12).

Luke 24:10 names her among the women who brought spices to the tomb and found it empty. The angels' message is delivered to "Mary Magdalene, Joanna, Mary the mother of James, and the other women with them." She is a witness to the resurrection, one of those whose testimony the apostles dismissed as "idle talk" (λῆρος, lēros). Yet Luke, the meticulous historian, records her name for posterity.

Cultural & Historical Context: Herod Antipas's court at Tiberias was Hellenized, politically sophisticated, and morally complex. Chuza's position would have provided Joanna with wealth, status, and access—and also required political maneuvering and ethical compromise. Her decision to align herself publicly with Jesus, a figure increasingly viewed with suspicion by the Herodian establishment, represents a significant personal and social risk. That her husband's name is preserved while her independent action is recorded suggests a woman of considerable agency within her marriage.

Modern Use & Middle-Name Pairings:
Joanna —the biblical form; elegant, strong, historically rich.
Joanna Grace —Yahweh has been gracious; her name doubled
Joanna Faith —the steward's wife who stewarded her resources for the kingdom
Joanne, Joan —English variants.
Chuza —not recommended for a child, but the story invites reflection on husbands who supported their wives' radical discipleship.

Susanna
The Lily, The Silent Servant

Original Language & Core Meaning: Σουσάννα (Sousanna), from the Hebrew שׁוֹשַׁנָּה (Shoshannah), meaning "lily" or "rose." The name evokes the flowers of the Song of Solomon, emblems of beauty and belovedness.

The Biblical Narrative: Susanna appears exactly once in Scripture, in a single verse: Luke 8:3. Her name is catalogued among the women who accompanied Jesus and the Twelve and who provided for them from their resources. That is all. No dialogue. No narrative. No miracle attributed to her or requested from her.

Yet her name is preserved. Luke, the careful historian, received and transmitted her identity across six decades. Someone remembered her. Someone ensured that "Susanna" would be spoken aloud whenever the Gospel was read. Her inclusion testifies that faithful, quiet service—financial support, logistical provision, behind-the-scenes sustenance—is itself a form of discipleship worthy of remembrance.

Cultural & Historical Context: Her Hebrew name suggests Jewish heritage. Her inclusion among independent women of means indicates financial resources. The very brevity of her mention, juxtaposed with the detailed accounts of others, models the reality of Christian community: not all are teachers, not all are evangelists, but all are remembered. The church's memory is capacious enough to include the lillies.

Modern Use & Middle-Name Pairings:
Susanna —the full biblical form; elegant, flowing, with the warmth of the Hebrew original.
Susanna Grace —lily of grace, quietly blooming
Susanna Joy —the joy of hidden service, known to God
Susan, Susanne, Susana —variants.

Lily —the English translation of her name.
Lily Faith —the flower that neither toils nor spins, yet is clothed in glory

---

Mary the Mother of James and Joses
The Faithful Witness

Original Language & Core Meaning: Μαρία ἡ Ἰακώβου καὶ Ἰωσῆ μήτηρ (*Maria hē Iakōbou kai Iōsē mētēr*)—"Mary the mother of James and Joses." Mark 15:40 also identifies her as "Mary the mother of James the younger and of Joses." Her identification through her sons indicates her honored status as the mother of known church leaders.

The Biblical Narrative: This Mary appears at the cross (Matthew 27:56; Mark 15:40), observing the crucifixion when the Twelve have scattered. She witnesses Jesus's burial (Mark 15:47). She purchases spices and prepares them to anoint his body (Luke 23:56). She returns to the tomb at dawn (Matthew 28:1; Mark 16:1). She encounters the angel who announces the resurrection (Matthew 28:5–7). She flees from the tomb with trembling and astonishment (Mark 16:8).

Her identification as mother of "James the younger" distinguishes her from Mary the mother of Jesus and Mary Magdalene. The epithet "younger" or "little" (μικροῦ, mikrou) may indicate physical stature or relative age; it places her sons within the leadership structure of the early Jerusalem church. Her faithful presence through crucifixion, burial, and empty tomb establishes her as a model of persevering discipleship.

Cultural & Historical Context: Maternal identification was conventional in a patriarchal society; a woman's honor derived significantly from her sons' achievements. That this Mary is named at all—and distinguished carefully from other Marys—indicates her prominence in the early Christian community. Her sons' leadership roles likely reflected her own faithful discipleship; the faith she transmitted to them was forged in her own costly following of Jesus.

Modern Use & Middle-Name Pairings:
Mary —again, the inexhaustible name.
Mary James —the traditional pairing honoring her sons
Mary Faith —the faith that watched and waited
Jacoba, Jacqueline —feminine forms of James.
Jacoba Grace —grace transmitted from mother to sons

Salome
The Peaceful, The Petitioner

Original Language & Core Meaning: Σαλώμη (Salōmē), the Greek form of the Hebrew שָׁלוֹם (*Shalom*), meaning "peace." She is the mother of the sons of Zebedee—James and John, the "sons of thunder."

The Biblical Narrative: Matthew 20:20–21 records her approaching Jesus with a bold request: "Say that these two sons of mine are to sit, one at your right hand and one at your left, in your kingdom." She kneels. She petitions. She asks for honor and authority for her boys.

It is an awkward moment. The other disciples are indignant. Jesus reframes greatness as servanthood. But he does not rebuke her love. He does not dismiss her ambition. He redirects it.

Mark 15:40 and 16:1 place Salome among the women at the cross and the empty tomb. This same mother, who sought earthly thrones for her sons, stands faithfully at the foot of an execution stake. She watches her teacher die. She brings spices to anoint a corpse. Her earlier request, so easily caricatured as pushy parenting, is revealed as the fierce love of a mother who believed her sons deserved a place in the Messiah's kingdom. She was wrong about the nature of the throne. She was not wrong about the worthiness of the King.

Cultural & Historical Context: Zebedee's sons left their father and their fishing nets to follow Jesus (Matthew 4:21–22). Their mother, Salome, apparently accompanied them or joined them later; her independent following of Jesus suggests a household where women as well as men responded to the call. Her request, scandalous in its presumption, reflects both maternal ambition and genuine conviction that Jesus was the coming King. The transformation from throne-seeker to tomb-visitor is the quiet arc of her discipleship.

Modern Use & Middle-Name Pairings:
Salome —the biblical name; bears the weight of her story.
Salome Peace —the meaning of her name, the fruit of her transformation
Salome Grace —grace that reframes ambition into service
Shalom —the Hebrew original.
Shalom Hope —the peace that comes from surrendered hope
Zebedee —not recommended; but the story invites reflection on family systems transformed by encounter with Christ.

Martha of Bethany
The Lady, The Confessor

Original Language & Core Meaning: Μάρθα (Martha), from the Aramaic מָרְתָא (Martha), the feminine form of מָר (mar), meaning "lord" or "master." Her name literally means "lady" or "mistress."

The Biblical Narrative: Martha appears in Luke 10:38–42 and John 11:1–44, two portraits that initially seem contradictory but together reveal a complete woman.

In Luke, Martha receives Jesus into her home. She is περισπᾶτο (perispato)—"distracted" or "dragged around" by her many tasks. She complains that her sister Mary sits listening while she works alone. Jesus responds: "Martha, Martha, you are anxious and troubled about many things, but one thing is necessary. Mary has chosen the good portion, which will not be taken away from her."

It sounds like a rebuke. It is, in fact, an invitation. Jesus speaks her name twice—the doubled address of tenderness. He does not despise her service; he desires her presence.

In John, her brother Lazarus lies dying. She sends word: "Lord, he whom you love is ill." Jesus delays. Lazarus dies. When Jesus finally arrives, Martha goes out to meet him while Mary remains in the house. And Martha speaks:

Κύριε, εἰ ἦς ὧδε, οὐκ ἂν ἀπέθανεν ὁ ἀδελφός μου (Kyrie, ei ēs hōde, ouk an apethanen ho adelphos mou)—"Lord, if you had been here, my brother would not have died."

It is not accusation. It is confession. She knows who Jesus is and what he could have done. Then Jesus declares: Ἐγώ εἰμι ἡ ἀνάστασις καὶ ἡ ζωή (Egō eimi hē anastasis kai hē zōē)—"I am the resurrection and the life." And he asks her: Πιστεύεις τοῦτο; (Pisteueis touto?)—"Do you believe this?"

Her response is the fullest Christological confession in the Gospels before the resurrection:

Ναί, Κύριε· ἐγὼ πεπίστευκα ὅτι σὺ εἶ ὁ Χριστὸς ὁ υἱὸς τοῦ θεοῦ ὁ εἰς τὸν κόσμον ἐρχόμενος (Nai, Kyrie; egō pepisteuka hoti sy ei ho Christos ho huios tou theou ho eis ton kosmon erchomenos)—"Yes, Lord; I believe that you are the Christ, the Son of God, he who is coming into the world."

Martha, distracted server, becomes Martha, definitive confessor.

Cultural & Historical Context: Bethany was a small village less than two miles from Jerusalem, on the eastern slope of the Mount of Olives. Martha's role as household head—receiving guests, managing hospitality, sending messengers—indicates either widowhood, singleness, or unusual authority within her family. The name "Martha" itself, meaning "lady" or "mistress," suggests she was known in her community as a woman of substance and capability. Her confession, deliberately echoing Peter's at Caesarea Philippi (Matthew 16:16), places her within the innermost circle of those who recognized Jesus's divine identity before the resurrection.

Modern Use & Middle-Name Pairings:
Martha —the biblical name; strong, classic, underappreciated.
Martha Grace —the lady who received grace upon grace
Martha Faith —the faith that confessed Christ before the empty tomb
Marta —the Spanish and Eastern European form.

Martina —the feminine diminutive; "little lady."
Martina Joy —the joy that transcends distraction

Mary of Bethany
The Listener, The Anointing Witness

Original Language & Core Meaning: Μαρία (Maria), the same Hebrew name borne by the mother of Jesus, Magdalene, and the mother of James. The name's proliferation testifies to its popularity and to the many women who bore it worthily.

The Biblical Narrative: Mary of Bethany appears in three episodes across Luke and John. In Luke 10:38–42, she sits at Jesus's feet listening to his teaching. The posture is that of a disciple; the place, at the teacher's feet, is the position of formal apprenticeship. Her sister Martha complains; Jesus defends Mary's choice.

In John 11:1–44, when Jesus arrives after Lazarus's death, Mary remains in the house while Martha goes out. When she finally comes to Jesus, she falls at his feet and speaks the same words Martha spoke: "Lord, if you had been here, my brother would not have died." Jesus, seeing her weeping, is deeply moved and weeps himself.

In John 12:1–8, six days before the Passover, Mary takes a pound of pure nard—an ointment so costly that Judas estimates its value at three hundred denarii, nearly a year's wages—and anoints Jesus's feet, wiping them with her hair. The house fills with fragrance. Judas objects. Jesus defends her: "Leave her alone, so that she may keep it for the day of my burial."

Mary understands what the disciples cannot grasp: Jesus is going to die. Her anointing is prophetic, liturgical, extravagantly loving. She does not wait to anoint a corpse; she honors her living Lord.

Cultural & Historical Context: A woman's hair was her glory (1 Corinthians 11:15); to unbind it in public was an act of intimacy

and vulnerability. Mary's use of her hair to wipe Jesus's feet—
already a task reserved for the lowest servant—compounded
the radical nature of her action. The value of the nard,
imported from the Himalayas, represents a life's savings or an
inheritance. Her act is not merely generous; it is economically
devastating. She gives everything.

Modern Use & Middle-Name Pairings:
Mary —again; each Mary carries distinct associations.
Mary Bethany —honoring her village and her hospitality
Mary Grace —the grace of extravagant love
Bethany —"house of affliction" or "house of figs"; the village
name as a given name.
Bethany Joy —the joy of sitting at the Teacher's feet
Bethany Faith —the faith that anointed before the burial

The Widow with Two Mites
The Poor Woman Who Gave Everything

Original Language & Core Meaning: Mark 12:41–44 and Luke 21:1–4 preserve her story. She is χήρα πτωχή (chēra ptōchē) —"a poor widow." Her name is unrecorded; her poverty is her identifier. Yet Jesus renames her. While others give from their abundance, she "out of her poverty has put in everything she had, all she had to live on." The Greek phrase is ὅλον τὸν βίον αὐτῆς (holon ton bion autēs)—her whole life, her entire livelihood.

The Biblical Narrative: Jesus sits opposite the treasury, watching people put money into the offering boxes. The rich contribute large sums. Then a poor widow comes and drops in two lepta—small bronze coins, the smallest currency in circulation, worth about 1/64 of a denarius (a day's wage).

Jesus calls his disciples and says: "Truly, I say to you, this poor widow has put in more than all those who are contributing to the offering box."

Her gift is quantitatively insignificant. Her gift is qualitatively total.

Cultural & Historical Context: The Jerusalem temple's treasury was located in the Court of Women, where thirteen trumpet-shaped collection boxes received offerings for various purposes. Widows occupied the most vulnerable position in ancient society, lacking male protection and often facing economic exploitation. This woman's gift of her last coins—everything she had to live on—is not merely generous but radically faithful. She gives God her survival, trusting God for her provision.

Modern Use & Middle-Name Pairings:
Penelope —from πήνη (pēnē), "weft" or "thread"; associated with weaving and domestic economy, yet also evoking "penny" through sound association.
Penelope Faith —the faith that gave everything
Penelope Grace —grace sufficient for the generous heart

10.
NAMES OF SISTERS IN THE EARLY CHURCH

The story of the early church is often told as a narrative of apostles, bishops, and male martyrs—Peter, Paul, Stephen, James. Yet beneath this familiar account lies another history, one written in feminine names that appear, often fleetingly, in the pages of Acts, the Epistles, and the earliest post-apostolic writings. These women were not peripheral figures. They were patrons who funded missions, leaders who hosted house churches, apostles who labored alongside Paul, prophets who spoke in the assembly, and witnesses who first proclaimed the resurrection. Their names—Mary, Prisca, Phoebe, Lydia, Junia, Tryphaena, Tryphosa, Persis, and others—are not mere footnotes. They are evidence of a movement in which women found, in the earliest decades, a remarkable scope for leadership and influence.

This chapter seeks to recover these women and place them in chronological order, insofar as the New Testament and early Christian literature allow. We will examine each name in its original language, uncover its core meaning, retell the biblical narrative in which it appears, situate the woman within her cultural and historical context, and consider the modern legacy of her name. What emerges is not a collection of isolated individuals but a network of women whose faith, resources, and labor shaped Christianity in its formative years.

Women in the Pauline Mission (c. 50–65 CE)

Lydia

Original Language: Greek: Λυδία (Lydia)
Core Meaning: "Lydian woman" (from Lydia, a region in western Asia Minor)

Biblical Narrative: Acts 16:14–15, 40 introduces Lydia as a "dealer in purple cloth" from the city of Thyatira. Hearing Paul's proclamation at a riverside prayer gathering in Philippi, "the Lord opened her heart to respond." She and her household were baptized, and she compelled Paul and his companions to stay in her home, which became the gathering place for the first European church.

Cultural and Historical Context: Lydia represents a class of independent, economically powerful women in the Roman world. Purple dye and purple-dyed cloth were luxury goods; Thyatira was renowned for its dyeing industry. As a merchant dealing in this trade, Lydia likely owned her own home and managed significant financial resources. Her ability to offer hospitality to an entire missionary team and to host a house church indicates both wealth and social standing. Susan Hylen notes that women of means in the Roman world were expected to use their resources for civic and familial benefit; Lydia's patronage of the Pauline mission exemplified this ideal.

Modern Use:
Lydia has remained consistently popular, ranking in the top 100 names in several English-speaking countries. Its classical roots and New Testament associations make it a perennial choice.

Middle-Name Pairings: Lydia Grace, Lydia Rose, Lydia Katherine, Lydia Mae, Lydia Nicole

---

Prisca (Priscilla)

Original Language: Latin: Prisca (feminine of priscus, "ancient," "venerable"); diminutive form Priscilla
Core Meaning: "Ancient," "venerable," "honorable"

Biblical Narrative: Prisca (Priscilla) appears alongside her husband Aquila in Acts 18, Romans 16:3–5, 1 Corinthians 16:19, and 2 Timothy 4:19. A Jewish couple from Rome expelled under Claudius, they settled in Corinth where they shared Paul's trade of tentmaking. They accompanied Paul to Ephesus, where they instructed Apollos, an eloquent Alexandrian Jew, "more accurately in the way of God" (Acts 18:26). Paul calls them his "fellow workers in Christ Jesus" and notes that they "risked their necks" for his life. A church met in their home.

Cultural and Historical Context: Significantly, Prisca is named before her husband in four of six New Testament references, unusual in a patriarchal culture and suggesting her prominence in the partnership. The couple were both tentmakers and missionaries, operating as an independent team. Their instruction of Apollos—a learned male teacher—demonstrates their theological competence and authority. That the church met in their home, not Aquila's alone, reflects Prisca's co-leadership. In the Roman world, married couples often operated as economic and social units; the Prisca-Aquila partnership exemplifies this pattern applied to Christian mission .

Modern Use:
Priscilla has enjoyed sustained popularity, particularly in evangelical circles. Prisca, the formal Latin form, is less common but increasingly used.

Middle-Name Pairings: Priscilla Anne, Priscilla Joy, Priscilla Hope, Prisca Jane, Prisca Faith

---

Phoebe

Original Language: Greek: Φοίβη (Phoibē)
Core Meaning: "Bright," "pure," "radiant" (associated with the moon and the Titan goddess Phoebe)

Biblical Narrative: Romans 16:1–2 introduces Phoebe with remarkable titles. She is designated a diakonos (διάκονος) of the church at Cenchreae, Corinth's eastern port. Paul commends her to the Roman believers and instructs them to "receive her in the Lord in a manner worthy of the saints and assist her in whatever matter she may have need of you, for she herself has been a prostatis (προστάτις) of many and of myself as well."

Cultural and Historical Context: Two Greek terms require careful attention. Diakonos can mean "servant" or "deacon"; in this context, given the formal reference to a specific church, it almost certainly denotes an official role. Prostatis is even more significant—it means "patron," "benefactor," or "guardian," describing someone who provides material support and legal advocacy. Phoebe was thus both a recognized minister in her congregation and a wealthy patron who supported Paul's work. That Paul entrusted her with the delivery and interpretation of his letter to the Romans—his most theologically weighty epistle—speaks to her competence and authority .

Modern Use:

Phoebe has seen a significant resurgence, ranking in the top 200 names in the United States and United Kingdom. Its pleasant sound and positive meaning combine with its strong biblical credentials.

Middle-Name Pairings: Phoebe Elizabeth, Phoebe Catherine, Phoebe Rose, Phoebe Jane, Phoebe Ann

---

Junia

Original Language: Latin: Junia (feminine form of Junius, a Roman family name)
Core Meaning: Associated with Juno, the queen of the Roman gods; "youthful" (possible derivation)

Biblical Narrative:
Romans 16:7 delivers Paul's greeting to "Andronicus and Junia, my kinsmen and my fellow prisoners, who are outstanding among the apostles, who also were in Christ before me."

Cultural and Historical Context: This verse has generated extensive scholarly discussion. Junia was universally recognized as a feminine name throughout antiquity; no example of a masculine "Junias" has been found. For centuries, however, translators rendered the name as the masculine "Junias" to avoid affirming a female apostle. Yet Paul explicitly states that Andronicus and Junia are "outstanding among the apostles"—meaning they were highly regarded *by* the apostles, or more likely, were themselves prominent *among* the apostles. Their imprisonment with Paul, their conversion before his, and their apostolic status place Junia among the highest ranks of early Christian leadership . Ben Witherington III notes that Paul's naming of Junia indicates her recognized authority in the early communities .

Modern Use:
Junia has been recovered in recent decades as a female name. It remains uncommon but is increasingly chosen by parents aware of its significance.

Middle-Name Pairings: Junia Rose, Junia Grace, Junia Claire, Junia Faith, Junia Kate

Tryphaena and Tryphosa

Original Language: Greek: Τρύφαινα (Tryphaina), Τρυφῶσα (Tryphōsa)

Core Meaning: Both derived from τρυφάω (tryphaō), "to live luxuriously" or "to live delicately"; the names suggest "dainty" or "delicate"

Biblical Narrative: Romans 16:12: "Greet Tryphaena and Tryphosa, those women who labor in the Lord."

Cultural and Historical Context: These two women, likely sisters or close relatives bearing cognate names, are described with the verb kopiaō (κοπιάω), which denotes labor to the point of weariness. This same verb is used of Paul's own apostolic work and of other ministerial leaders. J.B. Lightfoot suggested that the pairing of such similar names might indicate twin sisters, a phenomenon attested in both classical and biblical literature (compare Huz and Buz, Muppim and Huppim) . Both names appear in inscriptions of the Roman imperial household, suggesting these women may have been freedpersons or slaves connected to the palace. If so, their "labor in the Lord" took place in the very heart of the empire .

Modern Use:
Tryphaena and Tryphosa are extremely rare today, though Tryphena (a variant spelling) appears occasionally. Their complexity and obscurity limit modern usage.

Middle-Name Pairings: Not applicable for common modern use

Persis

Original Language: Greek: Περσίς (Persis)
Core Meaning: "Persian woman"

Biblical Narrative: Romans 16:12: "Greet Persis, the beloved, who has labored much in the Lord."

Cultural and Historical Context: Like Tryphaena and Tryphosa, Persis is described with kopiaō, the verb of apostolic labor. Paul adds the adjective "beloved" (ἀγαπητήν) and specifies that she has labored "much" (πολλά)—an intensifier not applied to the other women. Her name indicates ethnic origin or family heritage. She is the only woman in Romans 16 whose name is accompanied by a definite article, perhaps marking her as especially well-known to the Roman recipients. Like the others, her labor was not merely charitable work but ministry that Paul deemed worthy of apostolic recognition .

Modern Use:

Persis is rare, used occasionally in families with Persian heritage or among those seeking distinctive biblical names.

Middle-Name Pairings: Persis Grace, Persis Joy, Persis Elizabeth

---

Mary of Rome

Original Language: Hebrew: מִרְיָם (Miryam); Greek: Μαρία (Maria)
Core Meaning: "Beloved" or "bitterness"

Biblical Narrative: Romans 16:6: "Greet Mary, who has labored much for you."

Cultural and Historical Context: This Mary, distinct from the better-known Marys of the Gospels, labored among the Roman Christians. Paul's use of kopiaō places her in the same category of ministerial workers as Tryphaena, Tryphosa, and Persis. Nothing more is known of her, yet her preservation in this list testifies that her work was remembered and honored.

Modern Use:
See Mary, Mother of Jesus, above.

Middle-Name Pairings: Mary Elizabeth, Mary Katherine, Mary Grace

---

Euodia and Syntyche

Original Language: Greek: Εὐοδία (Euodia), Συντύχη (Syntychē)
Core Meaning: Euodia: "prosperous journey," "good path," "success"; Syntyche: "fortunate," "well-met," "with fate"

Biblical Narrative: Philippians 4:2–3: "I entreat Euodia and I entreat Syntyche to agree in the Lord. Yes, I ask you also, true companion, help these women, who have labored side by side with me in the gospel together with Clement and the rest of my fellow workers, whose names are in the book of life."

Cultural and Historical Context: These two women were Paul's coworkers in Philippi, the same city where Lydia had founded the church. Their disagreement threatened congregational unity, prompting Paul's public appeal. Yet significantly, Paul does not command them from above; he "entreats" them as equals. He affirms their past labor "side by side" with him—the verb *synathleō* (συναθλέω) suggests athletic competition, contending together as a team. Their names are written in the "book of life," Paul's assurance of their salvation despite their present conflict. The unnamed "true companion" (likely Epaphroditus or a Philippian leader) is instructed to "help these women," indicating they retained their standing in the community .

Modern Use:

Euodia (often anglicized as "Odilia" or left as Euodia) and Syntyche are rare. Euodia has seen occasional use; Syntyche remains extremely uncommon.

Middle-Name Pairings: Euodia Grace, Euodia Faith, Syntyche Hope (rare usage)

Apphia

Original Language: Greek: Ἀπφία (Apphia); a Phrygian name, diminutive form of Apphion
Core Meaning: "Productive," "fruitful," or possibly "beloved sister"

Biblical Narrative:
Philemon 1:2: "To Philemon our beloved fellow worker and Apphia our sister and Archippus our fellow soldier, and the church in your house."

Cultural and Historical Context: Apphia is almost certainly Philemon's wife and the hostess of the Colossian house church. Paul addresses her by name, separately from Philemon, indicating her recognized role. She is called "the sister" (τῇ ἀδελφῇ), a title denoting fellow believer and perhaps co-leader. In a household where the church gathered, Apphia would have shared responsibility for hospitality, teaching, and pastoral care. Her inclusion in the salutation of a personal letter demonstrates her significance .

Modern Use:
Apphia is rare, though "Apphia" appears occasionally. Some scholars note that the Phrygian name is linguistically related to "Appian" or "Apollos."

Middle-Name Pairings: Apphia Rose, Apphia Grace, Apphia Joy

Eunice and Lois

Original Language: Greek: Εὐνίκη (Eunikē), Λωΐς (Lōis)
Core Meaning: Eunice: "good victory"; Lois: from λωΐων (lōiōn), "more agreeable," "more desirable"

Biblical Narrative: 2 Timothy 1:5: "I am reminded of your sincere faith, a faith that dwelt first in your grandmother Lois and your mother Eunice and now, I am sure, dwells in you as well." Acts 16:1 notes that Timothy's mother was "a believing Jewish woman" while his father was Greek.

Cultural and Historical Context: Lois and Eunice represent the vital role of women in transmitting faith across generations. They were Jewish women who embraced Christianity, raising Timothy in the Scriptures from childhood (2 Timothy 3:15). In mixed marriages where the father was not a believer, the mother's religious formation became decisive. Paul's acknowledgment of their faith is not perfunctory—he places it at the foundation of Timothy's own sincerity. The Pastoral Epistles, often read as restrictive toward women, here preserve a powerful testimony to women's spiritual influence .

Modern Use:
Eunice was moderately popular in the early to mid-twentieth century but has declined. Lois enjoyed greater popularity mid-century and remains in occasional use.

Middle-Name Pairings: Eunice Claire, Eunice Marie, Lois Anne, Lois Catherine, Lois Elaine

---

Claudia

Original Language: Latin: Claudia
Core Meaning: Feminine form of Claudius, a Roman family name; possibly "lame" (from claudus)

Biblical Narrative: 2 Timothy 4:21: "Eubulus sends greetings to you, as do Pudens and Linus and Claudia and all the brothers."

Cultural and Historical Context: Claudia appears in the final greetings of 2 Timothy, likely from Rome. Tradition identifies her as a British woman, wife of Pudens, and mother of Linus (an early bishop of Rome). The name is common in Roman inscriptions and among the imperial household. Her presence among those sending greetings to Timothy indicates her membership in the Roman Christian community.

Modern Use:
Claudia has maintained steady, moderate popularity across decades. It is used throughout Europe and the Americas.

Middle-Name Pairings: Claudia Grace, Claudia Rose, Claudia Marie, Claudia Elizabeth, Claudia Jane

---

Tabitha (Dorcas)

Original Language: Aramaic: טְבִיתָא (Ṭəḇīṯā'); Greek: Δορκάς (Dorkas)
Core Meaning: "Gazelle"

Biblical Narrative: Acts 9:36–42 recounts the raising of Tabitha in Joppa. She is described as a disciple (μαθήτρια, mathētria—the only use of the feminine form in the New Testament) "full of good works and acts of charity." When she died, the widows showed Peter the garments she had made. Peter raised her, and "many believed in the Lord."

Cultural and Historical Context: Tabitha's designation as a mathētria places her among the formal followers of Jesus. Her charitable work—making tunics and garments—was not merely domestic but represented the diakonia (service) expected of disciples. Teresa Calpino notes that Tabitha and Lydia serve as models of early Christian women leaders whose economic productivity and patronage advanced the mission . The widows who mourned her were likely beneficiaries of her ministry, suggesting she led a network of charitable service.

Modern Use:

Tabitha enjoyed popularity in the 1990s and remains in moderate use. Dorcas is less common but persists in some traditional communities.

Middle-Name Pairings: Tabitha Rose, Tabitha Grace, Tabitha Jane, Dorcas Anne, Dorcas Elizabeth

---

Women in the Second Century and Non-Canonical Traditions

Thecla

Original Language: Greek: Θέκλα (Thekla)
Core Meaning: "Glory of God" (from θεός, theos, "God," and κλέος, kleos, "glory")

Biblical Narrative: Thecla does not appear in the canonical New Testament but is the heroine of the Acts of Paul and Thecla, a second-century apocryphal text. According to this account, Thecla was a young noblewoman from Iconium who heard Paul preach and abandoned her engagement to follow him. She endured persecution, baptized herself in the arena, and became a teacher and evangelist.

Cultural and Historical Context: Though legendary in its details, the Thecla tradition provides invaluable evidence for the roles women claimed in early Christianity. David R. Cartlidge notes that Thecla's fame in the second through fourth centuries "extended from Asia Minor to the eastern borders of the church, to the sands of Egypt and into Europe" . Her story reflects both the opportunities women found in the Christian movement and the opposition they faced. The Tertullian (c. 200) complained that some Asian churches claimed the Acts of Paul to authorize women's teaching and baptizing—indicating that Thecla was indeed used to justify women's ministry. Her cult persisted for centuries, and she was venerated as a proto-martyr and apostle .

Modern Use:
Thecla is rare in contemporary usage but persists in Orthodox communities and among those drawn to early Christian history.

Middle-Name Pairings: Thecla Rose, Thecla Grace, Thecla Marie, Anna Thecla

---

The Legacy of These Names

The women of the early church were not exceptions or anomalies. They were the norm. From the Galilean women who funded Jesus' ministry to the Roman patrons who hosted house churches, from the deacon Phoebe who delivered Paul's greatest letter to the apostle Junia who was imprisoned for the gospel, women were essential agents in Christianity's expansion.

Their names, preserved in the biblical text and early Christian memory, carry multiple legacies. Historically, they testify to a movement that, while operating within patriarchal structures, created unprecedented space for women's leadership. Theologically, they embody virtues—faith, hospitality, courage, perseverance—that transcend gender. Pastorally, they offer contemporary parents names rich with meaning and story.

To name a daughter Phoebe is to invoke the memory of a woman who carried the gospel across the Mediterranean. To name her Junia is to reclaim a legacy of apostolic authority too long obscured. To name her Lydia is to remember that the gospel first took root in Europe through the opened heart of a merchant woman. To name her Prisca is to honor the partnership of equals in ministry. To name her Tabitha is to affirm that service and charity are themselves works of discipleship worthy of remembrance.

These names, ancient in origin yet ever new, continue to speak. They echo from the house churches of Corinth and Rome, from the riverside at Philippi and the workshop in

Ephesus, from the pages of Paul's letters and the empty tomb on Easter morning. They are not merely historical artifacts. They are invitations—to know these women, to tell their stories, and to carry their legacy forward into each new generation.

12.
THINGS TO CONSIDER : CARRYING THE STORY FORWARD

The Weight of a Name

You have traveled with me through these pages, from the garden where Eve received the first name spoken by human lips, through the tents of the matriarchs and the battlefields of the judges, past the thrones of queens and the simple homes of Galilean women, into the house churches of Corinth and Rome where Phoebe and Prisca and Junia labored in the gospel. You have met women of courage and women of compromise, women whose faith shaped nations and women whose names survive in a single verse. You have learned the meanings buried in ancient syllables—Rachel's "ewe," Deborah's "bee," Tabitha's "gazelle"—and you have glimpsed the worlds those women inhabited.

Now comes the question that matters most: What do we do with all of this?

Beyond the Name Itself

The temptation, when choosing a biblical name, is to stop at the surface—to select Hannah because it sounds lovely, or

Abigail because it ranks highly on popularity lists, or Elizabeth because it feels classic and safe. These are not wrong reasons. Beauty and familiarity have their place. But if this book has accomplished anything, I hope it has shown that a biblical name is an entry point, not a destination.

To name a daughter Miriam is not merely to give her a Hebrew name that means "beloved" or "bitterness." It is to connect her to the prophetess who led Israel in song at the Red Sea, who watched over her baby brother Moses in the bulrushes, who spoke with authority alongside Aaron, who experienced both the heights of divine calling and the consequences of human frailty. It is to give her a story—a long, complicated, deeply human story—that she can grow into across a lifetime.

The names in this book are not labels. They are narratives compressed into syllables. They are invitations to explore, to question, to wrestle, and ultimately to claim. A child named Esther may one day ask, "Who was she, and why did you name me for her?" That question is the beginning of something sacred—a conversation about courage in the face of power, about identity hidden and revealed, about the providence that places each of us in a particular time for a particular purpose. "Perhaps you have come to the kingdom for such a time as this" becomes not merely a verse from an ancient scroll but a word spoken directly to her.

Telling the Story

And so the first responsibility of parents who choose a biblical name is simply this: tell the story. Not once, not formally, not as a lecture, but repeatedly, naturally, as part of the fabric of family life. Tell it at bedtime. Tell it at dinner. Tell it when the name appears in Scripture read at church. Tell it when she asks, and tell it when she doesn't.

Tell it with all its complexity. Do not sanitize Sarah's laughter or Rachel's jealousy or Rahab's profession. The Bible does not, and neither should we. Children need to know that the heroes of faith were not plastic saints but flesh-and-blood people who doubted and feared and failed—and whom God loved and used anyway. This is the gospel in miniature: that God's grace meets us not in our perfection but in our humanity.

Tell it with wonder. Help her imagine Miriam watching the basket among the reeds, Deborah palm tree under which Israel sought justice, Lydia listening by the riverside in Philippi. Help her see these women as real—as real as she is —and help her understand that the same God who called them calls her.

Living the Legacy

A name is not destiny. No child is condemned to relive the struggles of her namesake, nor is she guaranteed to embody that namesake's virtues. But a name can be a compass—a quiet, steady pointing toward a way of being in the world.

Abigail points toward wisdom and peacemaking, toward the courage to intervene when foolishness threatens destruction. Phoebe points toward service and patronage, toward using whatever resources we have for the sake of others. Prisca points toward partnership and teaching, toward the holy work of instructing those who need more accurate understanding. Tabitha points toward charity and craftsmanship, toward the dignity of making things with our hands for those in need.

These are not burdens to place on a child's shoulders. They are gifts—examples of women who lived faithfully in their own times and places, whose lives offer patterns we might prayerfully hope to see echoed in ours.

As she grows, look for the echoes. When she shows kindness to a friend, remember Ruth's loyalty to Naomi. When she speaks truth courageously, remember Esther's words before the king. When she perseveres through difficulty, remember Hannah's long wait for Samuel. Help her see herself in this great cloud of witnesses—not because she must become them, but because she walks the same path of faith they walked, toward the same God who met them in their need.

The Unnamed and the Unknown

We have spent these pages with named women, those whose identities Scripture preserved. But any honest conclusion must acknowledge the others—the countless women whose names were never recorded, whose stories were never told, whose lives and labor remain hidden in the margins of the text.

The daughter of Jephthah, who submitted to her father's tragic vow and whose name we will never know. The woman with the hemorrhage, who touched Jesus' garment in the crowd and was healed, and whose name is lost to history. The Syrophoenician woman who argued with Jesus for her daughter's healing, whose wit and persistence won the day, and whose name we do not have. The Samaritan woman at the well, who became the first evangelist to her village, and whose name is not given.

Their anonymity is not accidental. It reflects the reality that most women in most times have lived and died without their names recorded in any permanent record. It also serves as a reminder: the value of a life is not measured by whether a name appears in Scripture. These unnamed women were loved by God, known by Christ, and are remembered in heaven even if not on earth.

This matters when we think about naming. Some children will receive names from these pages—names with stories attached, names that carry centuries of memory. Others will receive names from family tradition, from cultural heritage, from parents' imaginations. Both are gifts. Both place a child within a story—family story, cultural story, human story. And both are opportunities to teach that every person, named or unnamed in any book, is known and loved by the God who calls each star by name.

A Name as Prayer

Here is a thought to carry with you: when you name a child, you are praying. You may not kneel. You may not close your eyes. But the act of choosing—of sifting through possibilities, of speaking possibilities aloud, of finally settling on this name for this child—is a form of prayer. It is hope made audible. It is blessing spoken before blessing can be understood.

To name a daughter Grace is to pray that she will know herself as recipient of unearned love. To name her Faith is to pray that trust in God will mark her days. To name her Hope is to pray that she will look toward the future with confidence, even in darkness. And to name her for one of the women in these pages—Sarah or Ruth or Mary or Lydia—is to pray that she will find in that ancient story a companion for her own.

Pray for her as you name her. Pray over her as you speak the name aloud for the first time. Pray that the virtues you see in her biblical namesake will take root in her heart. Pray that she will grow into the full meaning of her name, whatever it is. Pray that she will know herself as named by God, called by God, beloved of God.

The Story Continues

The Bible ends with a vision of a new heaven and a new earth, with the New Jerusalem descending like a bride adorned for her husband. It ends with a promise: "Behold, I am making all things new." It ends with an invitation: "Let the one who is thirsty come; let the one who desires take the water of life without price." And it ends with a name: "He who testifies to these things says, 'Surely I am coming soon.' Amen. Come, Lord Jesus!"

The story that began in a garden, with the naming of the first woman, ends in a city, with the Bride prepared for her Groom. Between those two moments, countless names have been spoken—some recorded in Scripture, most lost to human memory. But all are known. All are written, as Paul told the Philippians, in the book of life.

When you name a daughter from these pages, you add a verse to that continuing story. You take an ancient name— Miriam, Deborah, Esther, Phoebe, Junia—and you give it new flesh, new breath, new life in a new time. You become part of the great chain of transmission, passing forward not only a name but a story, not only a story but a faith.

The women in this book were real. They lived and loved and struggled and believed. They made mistakes and received grace. They were ordinary and extraordinary, faithful and faltering, exactly like us. And now, through the names they have left us, they speak still.

Listen for them. Tell their stories. Pray their names. And when the time comes, place your daughter's hand in theirs—across centuries, across cultures, across everything that seems to separate—and let her know that she is not alone. She walks a path others have walked before. She carries a light others have carried before. She bears a name that has been spoken before, in hope, in faith, in love.

And the one who spoke the first name—who called light from darkness and life from dust—speaks hers as well, with tenderness beyond all telling.

For you formed my inward parts; you knitted me together in my mother's womb. I praise you, for I am fearfully and wonderfully made. Wonderful are your works; my soul knows it very well.

—Psalm 139:13–14

APPENDICES

A.

INDEX OF NAMES (ALPHABETICAL)

A

Abi – 2 Kings 18:2; 2 Chronicles 29:1
Also known as Abijah; mother of King Hezekiah

Abigail – 1 Samuel 25:3–42; 2 Samuel 3:3
Wife of Nabal, then of David; mother of Chileab (Daniel)

Abihail – 1 Chronicles 2:29; Esther 2:15; 2 Chronicles 11:18
Multiple women: wife of Abishur; mother of Esther; wife of
Rehoboam

Abijah – 2 Chronicles 29:1
See Abi; mother of Hezekiah

Abishag – 1 Kings 1:3–4, 15; 2:17–22
Shunammite woman who cared for King David in his old age

Abital – 2 Samuel 3:4; 1 Chronicles 3:3
Wife of David; mother of Shephatiah

Achsah – Joshua 15:16–19; Judges 1:12–15
Daughter of Caleb; wife of Othniel

Adah – Genesis 4:19–23; Genesis 36:2–16
Two women: wife of Lamech (mother of Jabal and Jubal); wife
of Esau (mother of Eliphaz)

Ahlai – 1 Chronicles 2:31, 34–35
Daughter of Sheshan; mother of Attai (through her Egyptian
servant Jarha)

Ahinoam – 1 Samuel 14:50; 1 Samuel 25:43; 2 Samuel 3:2; 1
Chronicles 3:1
Two women: wife of Saul (mother of Michal); wife of David
(mother of Amnon)

Aholah – Ezekiel 23:4–5, 36, 44
Symbolic name for Samaria in Ezekiel's allegory

Aholibah – Ezekiel 23:4–5, 11, 22, 36, 44
Symbolic name for Jerusalem in Ezekiel's allegory

Aholibamah – Genesis 36:2–25
Wife of Esau; daughter of Anah

Anna – Luke 2:36–38
Prophetess in the temple who recognized Jesus as the
Messiah

Apphia – Philemon 1:2
Christian woman in Colossae; likely wife of Philemon

Atarah – 1 Chronicles 2:26
Wife of Jerahmeel; mother of Onam

Azubah – 1 Kings 22:42; 2 Chronicles 20:31; 1 Chronicles
2:18–19
Two women: mother of Jehoshaphat; wife of Caleb (daughter
of Jerioth)

B

Baara – 1 Chronicles 8:8
Wife of Shaharaim

Basemath – Genesis 26:34–35; 36:3–4, 10, 13, 17
Wife of Esau; daughter of Elon the Hittite

Bathsheba – 2 Samuel 11:2–12:24; 1 Kings 1:11–31; 2:13–19; 1 Chronicles 3:5
Wife of Uriah, then of David; mother of Solomon

Berenice – Acts 25:13, 23; 26:30
Daughter of Herod Agrippa I; sister of Herod Agrippa II

Bernice – See Berenice

Bilhah – Genesis 29:29; 30:3–7; 35:22, 25; 37:2; 46:25; 1 Chronicles 7:13
Rachel's servant; mother of Dan and Naphtali

Bithiah – 1 Chronicles 4:18
Daughter of Pharaoh; wife of Mered

C

Candace – Acts 8:27
Queen of the Ethiopians; her treasurer was baptized by Philip

Chloe – 1 Corinthians 1:11
Prominent woman in Corinth or Ephesus; head of a household

Claudia – 2 Timothy 4:21
Christian woman in Rome sending greetings to Timothy

Cozbi – Numbers 25:6–18
Midianite woman killed by Phinehas

D

Damaris – Acts 17:34
Athenian woman who believed after Paul's Areopagus speech

Deborah – Genesis 35:8; Judges 4:4–5:31
Two women: Rebekah's nurse; prophetess and judge of Israel

Delilah – Judges 16:4–20
Woman who betrayed Samson to the Philistines

Dinah – Genesis 30:21; 34:1–31; 46:15
Daughter of Jacob and Leah

Dorcas – Acts 9:36–42
See Tabitha; disciple in Joppa known for good works

Druzilla – Acts 24:24
Daughter of Herod Agrippa I; wife of Felix

E

Eglah – 2 Samuel 3:5; 1 Chronicles 3:3
Wife of David; mother of Ithream

Elisheba – Exodus 6:23
Wife of Aaron; daughter of Amminadab

Elizabeth – Luke 1:5–60
Wife of Zechariah; mother of John the Baptist

Ephah – 1 Chronicles 2:46
Concubine of Caleb; mother of Haran, Moza, and Gazez

Ephrath – 1 Chronicles 2:19, 50; 4:4
Wife of Caleb; mother of Hur

Esther – Esther 2:7–9:32
Also known as Hadassah; Jewish queen of Persia who saved
her people

Eunice – 2 Timothy 1:5; Acts 16:1
Mother of Timothy; daughter of Lois

Euodia – Philippians 4:2–3
Christian woman in Philippi; Paul's coworker

Eve – Genesis 3:20; 4:1–2, 25; 2 Corinthians 11:3; 1 Timothy
2:13
First woman; mother of all living

G

Gomer – Hosea 1:3–9
Wife of Hosea; daughter of Diblaim; mother of Jezreel, Lo-
Ruhamah, and Lo-Ammi

H

Hagar – Genesis 16:1–16; 21:9–21; 25:12; Galatians 4:24–25
Sarah's Egyptian servant; mother of Ishmael

Haggith – 2 Samuel 3:4; 1 Kings 1:5, 11; 2:13; 1 Chronicles 3:2
Wife of David; mother of Adonijah

Hammolecheth – 1 Chronicles 7:17–18
Daughter of Machir; sister of Gilead

Hamutal – 2 Kings 23:31; 24:18; Jeremiah 52:1
Wife of Josiah; mother of Jehoahaz and Zedekiah

Hannah – 1 Samuel 1:2–2:21
Wife of Elkanah; mother of Samuel

Hazelelponi – 1 Chronicles 4:3
Daughter of Etam

Helah – 1 Chronicles 4:5, 7
Wife of Ashhur; mother of Zereth, Izhar, and Ethnan

Hephzibah – 2 Kings 21:1; Isaiah 62:4
Wife of Hezekiah; mother of Manasseh; also a symbolic name
for restored Jerusalem

Herodias – Matthew 14:3–11; Mark 6:17–28; Luke 3:19
Wife of Herod Philip, then of Herod Antipas; mother of
Salome

Hodesh – 1 Chronicles 8:8–9
Wife of Shaharaim

Hoglah – Numbers 26:33; 27:1; 36:11; Joshua 17:3
Daughter of Zelophehad; received inheritance

I

Iscah – Genesis 11:29
Daughter of Haran; sister of Lot and Milcah

Ishbah – 1 Chronicles 4:17
Mother of Eshtemoa

Ittah – See Jael

J

Jaakobah – 1 Chronicles 4:36 (possibly male; included with caution)

Jael – Judges 4:17–22; 5:6, 24–27
Wife of Heber the Kenite; killed Sisera

Jecoliah – 2 Kings 15:2; 2 Chronicles 26:3
Wife of Amaziah; mother of Uzziah (Azariah)

Jedidah – 2 Kings 22:1
Wife of Amon; mother of Josiah

Jehoaddin – 2 Kings 14:2; 2 Chronicles 25:1
Wife of Joash; mother of Amaziah

Jehosheba – 2 Kings 11:2; 2 Chronicles 22:11
Daughter of King Joram; sister of Ahaziah; wife of Jehoiada; saved Joash

Jehudijah – 1 Chronicles 4:18
Wife of Mered; mother of Jered, Heber, and Jekuthiel

Jemimah – Job 42:14
Daughter of Job; born after his restoration

Jeriot – 1 Chronicles 2:18 (possibly male; included with
caution)

Jerusha – 2 Kings 15:33; 2 Chronicles 27:1
Wife of Uzziah; mother of Jotham

Jezebel – 1 Kings 16:31; 18:4–19:2; 21:5–25; 2 Kings 9:7–37;
Revelation 2:20
Wife of Ahab; also a symbolic name in Revelation

Joanna – Luke 8:3; 24:10
Wife of Chuza, Herod's steward; follower of Jesus

Judith – Genesis 26:34
Wife of Esau; daughter of Beeri the Hittite

Julia – Romans 16:15
Christian woman in Rome greeted by Paul

Junia – Romans 16:7
Female apostle; imprisoned with Paul

K

Keren-happuch – Job 42:14
Daughter of Job; born after his restoration

Keziah – Job 42:14
Daughter of Job; born after his restoration

L

Leah – Genesis 29:16–31:33; 33:1–7; 34:1; 49:31; Ruth 4:11
Wife of Jacob; mother of Reuben, Simeon, Levi, Judah, Issachar, Zebulun, and Dinah

Lo-Ammi – Hosea 1:9
Symbolic daughter of Hosea; name means "not my people"

Lo-Ruhamah – Hosea 1:6, 8
Symbolic daughter of Hosea; name means "not loved"

Lois – 2 Timothy 1:5
Grandmother of Timothy; mother of Eunice

Lydia – Acts 16:14–15, 40
Purple cloth merchant in Philippi; first European convert

M

Maacah – 2 Samuel 3:3; 1 Kings 15:13; 2 Chronicles 11:20–22; 13:2; 15:16
Multiple women: wife of David (mother of Absalom); mother of Abijam; concubine of Caleb; wife of Machir

Mahalah – 1 Chronicles 7:18
Daughter of Hammolecheth; sister of Ishhod, Abiezer, and Shemida

Mahlah – Numbers 26:33; 27:1–7; 36:1–12; Joshua 17:3–4
Daughter of Zelophehad; received inheritance

Mara – Ruth 1:20
Name Naomi called herself meaning "bitter"

Martha – Luke 10:38–42; John 11:1–39; 12:2
Sister of Mary and Lazarus; follower of Jesus

Mary – Multiple New Testament references
Several women:
        - Mary, mother of Jesus – Matthew 1–2; Luke 1–2;
        John 2; Acts 1:14
        - Mary Magdalene – All Gospels; Luke 8:2; John
        20:1–18
        - Mary of Bethany – Luke 10:38–42; John 11–12
        - Mary of Clopas – John 19:25
        - Mary of Rome – Romans 16:6
        - Mary, mother of James and Joseph – Matthew
        27:56; Mark 15:40
        - Mary, mother of John Mark – Acts 12:12

Matred – Genesis 36:39; 1 Chronicles 1:50
Daughter of Mezahab; mother of Mehetabel

Mehetabel – Genesis 36:39; 1 Chronicles 1:50; Nehemiah 6:10
Two women: wife of Hadar; daughter of Delaiah

Meshullemeth – 2 Kings 21:19
Wife of Manasseh; mother of Amon

Michal – 1 Samuel 14:49; 18:20–19:17; 25:44; 2 Samuel 3:13–
16; 6:16–23; 1 Chronicles 15:29
Daughter of Saul; wife of David

Milcah – Genesis 11:29; 22:20–23; 24:15, 24, 47; Numbers
26:33
Two women: daughter of Haran; sister of Iscah; wife of Nahor;
daughter of Zelophehad

Miriam – Exodus 15:20–21; Numbers 12:1–15; 20:1; 26:59;
Deuteronomy 24:9; 1 Chronicles 6:3; Micah 6:4

Sister of Moses and Aaron; prophetess

N

Naamah – Genesis 4:22; 1 Kings 14:21, 31; 2 Chronicles 12:13
Two women: daughter of Lamech and Zillah; wife of Solomon; mother of Rehoboam

Naarah – 1 Chronicles 4:5–6
Wife of Ashhur; mother of Ahuzzam, Hepher, Temeni, and Haahashtari

Naomi – Ruth 1:2–4:17
Wife of Elimelech; mother-in-law of Ruth

Nephish – 1 Chronicles 5:19 (possibly male; included with caution)

Noadiah – Nehemiah 6:14; 1 Chronicles 3:24 (prophetess; also possibly male)
Prophetess who opposed Nehemiah

O

Oholah – See Aholah

Oholibah – See Aholibah

Orpah – Ruth 1:4–14
Moabite wife of Chilion; sister-in-law of Ruth

P

Peninnah – 1 Samuel 1:2–4
Wife of Elkanah; rival of Hannah

Persis – Romans 16:12
Christian woman in Rome; Paul's coworker

Peter's Wife – Matthew 8:14; Mark 1:30; Luke 4:38; 1
Corinthians 9:5
Unnamed; mentioned as mother-in-law and as accompanied
by Peter

Phoebe – Romans 16:1–2
Deacon of Cenchreae; patron of Paul

Pilate's Wife – Matthew 27:19
Unnamed; warned Pilate about Jesus

Prisca (Priscilla) – Acts 18:2–26; Romans 16:3–4; 1 Corinthians
16:19; 2 Timothy 4:19
Wife of Aquila; teacher of Apollos

Puah – Exodus 1:15–21
Hebrew midwife who feared God

R

Rachel – Genesis 29–35; 46:19–25; Ruth 4:11; Jeremiah 31:15;
Matthew 2:18
Wife of Jacob; mother of Joseph and Benjamin

Rahab – Joshua 2:1–21; 6:17–25; Matthew 1:5; Hebrews 11:31;
James 2:25
Prostitute of Jericho who hid the spies; ancestor of Jesus

Rebekah – Genesis 22:23; 24–29; 49:31; Romans 9:10
Wife of Isaac; mother of Jacob and Esau

Reumah – Genesis 22:24
Concubine of Nahor; mother of Tebah, Gaham, Tahash, and Maacah

Rhoda – Acts 12:13–15
Servant girl in Mary's house who announced Peter's release

Rizpah – 2 Samuel 3:7; 21:8–14
Concubine of Saul; mother of Armoni and Mephibosheth

Ruth – Book of Ruth; Matthew 1:5
Moabite wife of Boaz; great-grandmother of David

S

Salome – Mark 15:40; 16:1; Matthew 27:56
Follower of Jesus; possibly mother of James and John

Salome (daughter of Herodias) – Matthew 14:6–11; Mark 6:22–28
Daughter of Herodias; danced for Herod

Samaritan Woman – John 4:4–42
Unnamed woman at the well who believed

Sapphira – Acts 5:1–10
Wife of Ananias; died for lying to the Holy Spirit

Sarah (Sarai) – Genesis 11–23; Isaiah 51:2; Romans 4:19; 9:9; Hebrews 11:11; 1 Peter 3:6
Wife of Abraham; mother of Isaac

Selah – Possibly a musical term; not a woman

Shelomith – Leviticus 24:11; 1 Chronicles 3:19; 2 Chronicles 11:20; Ezra 8:10
Multiple women: daughter of Dibri; daughter of Zerubbabel; daughter of Rehoboam

Sheerah – 1 Chronicles 7:24
Daughter of Ephraim; built Lower and Upper Beth-horon and Uzzen-sheerah

Shimeath – 2 Kings 12:21; 2 Chronicles 24:26
Ammonite mother of Jozachar (Zabad)

Shomer – 2 Kings 12:21 (possibly male; mother of Jehozabad)

Shua – 1 Chronicles 2:3; 7:32
Two women: daughter of Heber; wife of Judah (unnamed in Genesis 38)

Shulammite – Song of Solomon 6:13
Beloved in the Song of Songs

Sintyche – See Syntyche

Sitrah – See Zilpah (not biblical; confusion)

Susanna – Luke 8:3
Follower of Jesus who provided for him

Syntyche – Philippians 4:2–3
Christian woman in Philippi; Paul's coworker

T

Tabitha – Acts 9:36–42
Also known as Dorcas; disciple in Joppa raised by Peter*

Tahpenes – 1 Kings 11:19–20
Queen of Egypt; sister of Hadad's wife

Tamar – Genesis 38:6–30; Ruth 4:12; 1 Chronicles 2:4; 2
Samuel 13:1–32; 14:27; 1 Chronicles 3:9
Three women: daughter-in-law of Judah; daughter of David;
daughter of Absalom

Taphath – 1 Kings 4:11
Daughter of Solomon; wife of Ben-abinadab

Thecla – Not in canonical Scripture; Acts of Paul and Thecla
Early Christian woman; venerated as a saint

The Woman Clothed with the Sun – Revelation 12:1–17
Symbolic woman in Revelation

Tirzah – Numbers 26:33; 27:1; 36:11; Joshua 17:3
Daughter of Zelophehad; received inheritance

Tryphaena – Romans 16:12
Christian woman in Rome; Paul's coworker

Tryphosa – Romans 16:12
Christian woman in Rome; Paul's coworker

U

Unnamed Women Throughout Scripture – Too numerous to
list individually, including:

- The woman with the issue of blood (Matthew 9:20–22; Mark 5:25–34; Luke 8:43–48)
- The Syrophoenician woman (Matthew 15:21–28; Mark 7:24–30)
- The bent woman healed on the Sabbath (Luke 13:10–17)
- Jephthah's daughter (Judges 11:29–40)
- The Levite's concubine (Judges 19–20)
- The widow of Zarephath (1 Kings 17:8–24)
- The Shunammite woman (2 Kings 4:8–37)
- And many others

V

Vashti – Esther 1:9–22; 2:1–4, 17
Queen of Persia; deposed by Ahasuerus

W

Widow's Mite – Mark 12:41–44; Luke 21:1–4
Unnamed poor widow who gave all she had

Woman at the Well – See Samaritan Woman

Woman with the Alabaster Jar – Matthew 26:6–13; Mark 14:3–9; Luke 7:36–50; John 12:1–8
Unnamed woman (identified as Mary of Bethany in John) who anointed Jesus

---

Z

Zebidah – 2 Kings 23:36

Wife of Josiah; mother of Jehoiakim

Zelophehad's Daughters – Numbers 26:33; 27:1–11; 36:1–12;
Joshua 17:3–6
Mahlah, Noah, Hoglah, Milcah, and Tirzah

Zeresh – Esther 5:10–14; 6:13
Wife of Haman

Zeruah – 1 Kings 11:26
Mother of Jeroboam*

Zeruiah – 1 Samuel 26:6; 2 Samuel 2:13, 18; 3:39; 8:16; 16:9–
10; 17:25; 19:21–22; 21:17; 23:18, 37; 1 Kings 1:7; 2:5, 22; 1
Chronicles 2:16; 11:6, 39; 18:12; 26:28; 27:24
Sister of David; mother of Abishai, Joab, and Asahel

Zibiah – 2 Kings 12:1; 2 Chronicles 24:1
Wife of Ahaziah; mother of Joash

Zillah – Genesis 4:19–23
Wife of Lamech; mother of Tubal-cain and Naamah

Zilpah – Genesis 29:24; 30:9–13; 35:26; 37:2; 46:18
Leah's servant; mother of Gad and Asher

Zipporah – Exodus 2:21–22; 4:25–26; 18:2–6
Daughter of Jethro/Reuel; wife of Moses

Note on Compilation

This index includes all named women in the canonical
Protestant Bible (66 books), along with several unnamed
women of significance and one figure from early Christian
tradition (Thecla) whose name appears in non-canonical

literature. Women whose names appear only in genealogies are included. In cases where names may refer to either males or females, caution has been noted. Alternate spellings and variant forms are cross-referenced.

The total number of named women in the Protestant canon is approximately 170, though this number varies slightly depending on whether certain individuals are counted separately or as duplicates across different books. When including unnamed women of significance, the total number of identifiable female figures exceeds 200.

"Her children rise up and call her blessed."
— Proverbs 31:28

B.
INDEX OF NAMES BY BIBLICAL BOOKS

This index organizes every named woman in the Bible according to the book in which her name first appears or where her primary story is located. Some women appear in multiple books; in such cases, they are listed under the book where their narrative is most developed, with cross-references to other appearances. Symbolic figures (such as the "woman clothed with the sun" in Revelation) are included where they function as named figures, even when the name is metaphorical. The index follows the canonical order of the Protestant Bible, with the Old Testament arranged according to the Hebrew canon's ordering of Law, Prophets, and Writings.

THE OLD TESTAMENT

Genesis
- Eve (Chavah) — Genesis 3:20
- Adah (wife of Lamech) — Genesis 4:19–23
- Zillah — Genesis 4:19–22
- Sarai (later Sarah) — Genesis 11:29–23:20
- Milcah (daughter of Haran) — Genesis 11:29; 22:20–23
- Iscah — Genesis 11:29
- Sarah (formerly Sarai) — Genesis 17:15–23:20
- Hagar — Genesis 16; 21:8–21
- Rebekah — Genesis 24–27

- Keturah — Genesis 25:1–4
- Deborah (Rebekah's nurse) — Genesis 35:8
- Rachel — Genesis 29–35
- Leah — Genesis 29–35
- Zilpah — Genesis 29:24; 30:9–13
- Bilhah — Genesis 29:29; 30:1–8
- Dinah — Genesis 30:21; 34
- Tamar (daughter-in-law of Judah) — Genesis 38
- Asenath — Genesis 41:45, 50–52; 46:20
- Potiphera's daughter (Asenath; included here as named figure)
- Shelah's wife (unnamed in Genesis, but Tamar is the primary figure)

Exodus
- Jochebed — Exodus 6:20; Numbers 26:59
- Miriam — Exodus 15:20–21; Numbers 12; 20:1; Deuteronomy 24:9
- Zipporah — Exodus 2:21–22; 4:24–26; 18:2–6
- Puah (midwife) — Exodus 1:15–21
- Shiphrah (midwife) — Exodus 1:15–21
- Elisheba — Exodus 6:23

Leviticus
- (No named women)

Numbers
- Shelomith (daughter of Dibri) — Leviticus 24:11 (cross-reference; primary in Numbers)
- Salome (not in Numbers; see Mark)
- Cozbi — Numbers 25:6–18
- Hoglah — Numbers 26:33; 27:1–11; 36:1–12
- Mahlah — Numbers 26:33; 27:1–11; 36:1–12
- Milcah (daughter of Zelophehad) — Numbers 26:33; 27:1–11; 36:1–12
- Noah (daughter of Zelophehad) — Numbers 26:33; 27:1–11; 36:1–12

- Tirzah — Numbers 26:33; 27:1–11; 36:1–12
- Serah (daughter of Asher) — Numbers 26:46; Genesis 46:17

Deuteronomy
- (No new named women; references to Miriam, others from previous books)

Joshua
- Rahab — Joshua 2; 6:17–25
- Achsah — Joshua 15:16–19; Judges 1:12–15

Judges
- Deborah (prophetess and judge) — Judges 4–5
- Jael — Judges 4:17–22; 5:24–27
- Sisera's mother (unnamed in text, mentioned in Deborah's song)
- Gideon's concubine (mother of Abimelech; named in some traditions but not in text)
- Abimelech's mother (unnamed in text)
- Jotham's mother (unnamed in text)
- Delilah — Judges 16
- Micah's mother — Judges 17:1–4
- Jephthah's daughter (unnamed in text; often called "Seila" in tradition)
- Jephthah's mother (unnamed in text)
- Samson's mother (unnamed in text; referred to as "Manoah's wife")
- Naamah (mother of Abimelech?; not to be confused with Naamah the Ammonite)

Ruth
- Naomi — Ruth 1–4
- Ruth — Ruth 1–4
- Orpah — Ruth 1:4–14

- Boaz's mother (Rahab, according to Matthew 1:5; see Joshua)
- Perez's mother (Tamar; see Genesis)

1 Samuel

- Hannah — 1 Samuel 1–2
- Peninnah — 1 Samuel 1:2–7
- Michal — 1 Samuel 14:49; 18:20–29; 19:11–17; 25:44; 2 Samuel 3:13–16; 6:16–23
- Merab — 1 Samuel 14:49; 18:17–19
- Abigail (wife of Nabal, later wife of David) — 1 Samuel 25; 2 Samuel 3:3
- Ahinoam (of Jezreel) — 1 Samuel 25:43; 27:3; 30:5; 2 Samuel 2:2; 3:2
- Maacah (daughter of Talmai, wife of David) — 1 Samuel 27:3; 2 Samuel 3:3
- Rizpah — 2 Samuel 3:7; 21:8–14
- Bathsheba — 2 Samuel 11–12; 1 Kings 1–2; 1 Chronicles 3:5 (where she is called Bathshua)
- Tamar (daughter of David) — 2 Samuel 13
- Abishag — 1 Kings 1:1–4; 2:17–22

2 Samuel

- (See 1 Samuel for most; additionally:)
- Zeruiah (David's sister; mother of Joab, Abishai, Asahel) — 2 Samuel 2:18; 1 Chronicles 2:16
- Abigail (David's sister) — 2 Samuel 17:25; 1 Chronicles 2:16–17
- The wise woman of Tekoa — 2 Samuel 14
- The medium of En-dor — 1 Samuel 28 (sometimes called "witch of Endor")

1 Kings

- Abishag (see 2 Samuel)
- Bathsheba (see 2 Samuel)
- Naamah (the Ammonite; mother of Rehoboam) — 1 Kings 14:21, 31; 2 Chronicles 12:13

- Maacah (daughter of Abishalom, mother of Asa) — 1 Kings 15:2, 10–13; 2 Chronicles 11:20–22; 15:16
- Jezebel — 1 Kings 16–21; 2 Kings 9
- Zeruah (mother of Jeroboam) — 1 Kings 11:26
- The widow of Zarephath — 1 Kings 17:8–24
- The Shunammite woman — 2 Kings 4:8–37; 8:1–6
- Athaliah — 2 Kings 11; 2 Chronicles 22–23

2 Kings

- The Shunammite woman (see 1 Kings)
- Huldah (prophetess) — 2 Kings 22:14–20; 2 Chronicles 34:22–28
- Naaman's wife's servant girl — 2 Kings 5:2–4
- Athaliah (see 1 Kings)
- Jehosheba (or Jehoshabeath) — 2 Kings 11:2; 2 Chronicles 22:11
- Zibiah — 2 Kings 12:1; 2 Chronicles 24:1
- Jecoliah — 2 Kings 15:2; 2 Chronicles 26:3
- Jerusha — 2 Kings 15:33; 2 Chronicles 27:1
- Abi (or Abijah) — 2 Kings 18:2; 2 Chronicles 29:1
- Hephzibah — 2 Kings 21:1
- Meshullemeth — 2 Kings 21:19
- Jedidah — 2 Kings 22:1
- Hamutal — 2 Kings 23:31; 24:18; Jeremiah 52:1
- Zebidah — 2 Kings 23:36
- Nehushta — 2 Kings 24:8

1 Chronicles

- Adam (genealogies; see Genesis)
- Eve (see Genesis)
- Sarah (see Genesis)
- Hagar (see Genesis)
- Keturah (see Genesis)
- Zilpah (see Genesis)
- Bilhah (see Genesis)
- Rachel (see Genesis)
- Leah (see Genesis)

- Dinah (see Genesis)
- Tamar (see Genesis)
- Asenath (see Genesis)
- Jochebed (see Exodus)
- Miriam (see Exodus)
- Zipporah (see Exodus)
- Elisheba (see Exodus)
- Serah (see Numbers)
- Shelomith (see Numbers)
- Mahlah (see Numbers)
- Noah (see Numbers)
- Hoglah (see Numbers)
- Milcah (see Numbers)
- Tirzah (see Numbers)
- Rahab (see Joshua)
- Achsah (see Joshua)
- Naomi (see Ruth)
- Ruth (see Ruth)
- Hannah (see 1 Samuel)
- Peninnah (see 1 Samuel)
- Michal (see 1 Samuel)
- Merab (see 1 Samuel)
- Abigail (see 1 Samuel)
- Ahinoam (see 1 Samuel)
- Maacah (see 1 Samuel)
- Rizpah (see 1 Samuel)
- Bathsheba (see 1 Samuel)
- Zeruiah (see 2 Samuel)
- Abigail (David's sister; see 2 Samuel)
- Tamar (see 2 Samuel)
- Maacah (see 1 Kings)
- Jezebel (see 1 Kings)
- Athaliah (see 1 Kings)
- Jehosheba (see 2 Kings)
- Zibiah (see 2 Kings)
- Jecoliah (see 2 Kings)
- Jerusha (see 2 Kings)

- Abi (see 2 Kings)
- Hephzibah (see 2 Kings)
- Meshullemeth (see 2 Kings)
- Jedidah (see 2 Kings)
- Hamutal (see 2 Kings)
- Zebidah (see 2 Kings)
- Nehushta (see 2 Kings)
- Ephah (concubine of Caleb) — 1 Chronicles 2:46
- Gazer (servant of Sheshan) — 1 Chronicles 2:34–35 (named Jarha; wife unnamed)
- Azubah (wife of Caleb) — 1 Chronicles 2:18–19
- Jerioth — 1 Chronicles 2:18
- Ephrath — 1 Chronicles 2:19; 4:4
- Helah — 1 Chronicles 4:5
- Naarah — 1 Chronicles 4:5–6
- Hammolecheth — 1 Chronicles 7:18
- Maachah (various; see notes)
- Abihail — 1 Chronicles 2:29
- Abigail (see above; multiple)
- The daughters of Zelophehad (see Numbers)

2 Chronicles
- (Most names appear in Kings or Chronicles; additionally:)
- Maacah (see 1 Kings and 2 Chronicles 11–15)
- Athaliah (see 1 Kings)
- Jehoshabeath (see 2 Kings as Jehosheba)
- Zibiah (see 2 Kings)
- Jecoliah (see 2 Kings)
- Jerusha (see 2 Kings)
- Abijah (mother of Hezekiah; see 2 Kings as Abi)
- Hephzibah (see 2 Kings)
- Meshullemeth (see 2 Kings)
- Jedidah (see 2 Kings)
- Hamutal (see 2 Kings)
- Zebidah (see 2 Kings)
- Nehushta (see 2 Kings)

Ezra

- (No named women)

Nehemiah

- (No named women)

Esther

- Vashti — Esther 1–2
- Esther (Hadassah) — Esther 2–9
- Zeresh — Esther 5:10–14; 6:13

Job

- Job's wife (unnamed in text)
- Jemimah — Job 42:14
- Keziah — Job 42:14
- Keren-happuch — Job 42:14
- Dinah (see Genesis; not in Job)

Psalms

- (No named women, though women are referenced)

Proverbs

- Wisdom (personified as feminine) — Proverbs 1–9
- The woman of valor (Eshet Chayil) — Proverbs 31:10–31
- Lemuel's mother — Proverbs 31:1–9

Ecclesiastes

- (No named women)

Song of Solomon (Song of Songs)

- The Shulammite — Song of Solomon 6:13
- The daughters of Jerusalem (collective, not individuals)

Isaiah

- Isaiah's wife (the prophetess) — Isaiah 8:3
- Hephzibah (symbolic) — Isaiah 62:4
- Beulah (symbolic) — Isaiah 62:4
- Daughter of Zion (personified) — throughout
- Virgin of Israel (personified) — throughout

Jeremiah

- Hamutal (see 2 Kings)
- Nehushta (see 2 Kings)
- Anathoth women (unnamed mourners) — Jeremiah 9:17–20
- The queen of heaven (deity, not a woman)

Lamentations

- Daughter of Zion (personified) — throughout
- Daughter of Jerusalem (personified) — throughout
- Daughter of Edom (personified) — Lamentations 4:21–22

Ezekiel

- Oholah (symbolic; Samaria) — Ezekiel 23
- Oholibah (symbolic; Jerusalem) — Ezekiel 23
- Ezekiel's wife — Ezekiel 24:15–18

Daniel

- Susanna — Daniel 13 (in the Apocrypha/Deuterocanon)
- Daniel's companions (no named women in Hebrew portion)

Hosea

- Gomer — Hosea 1–3
- Lo-ruhamah (symbolic name; Hosea's daughter) — Hosea 1:6–8
- Hosea's wife (Gomer; see above)

Joel

- (No named women)

Amos

- (No named women)

Obadiah

- (No named women)

Jonah

- (No named women)

Micah

- (No named women)

Nahum

- (No named women)

Habakkuk

- (No named women)

Zephaniah

- (No named women)

Haggai

- (No named women)

Zechariah

- (No named women)

Malachi

- (No named women; "daughter of a foreign god" referenced)

Tobit

- Anna (wife of Tobit) — Tobit 1–14
- Sarah (daughter of Raguel) — Tobit 3–12
- Deborah (nurse of Sarah) — Tobit 1:8 (possibly same as Genesis Deborah?)

Judith

- Judith — Judith 8–16

Wisdom of Solomon

- Wisdom (personified as feminine) — throughout

Sirach (Ecclesiasticus)

- (No named women, though women are discussed)

Baruch

- (No named women)

1 Maccabees

- Mattathias's mother (unnamed)
- The mother and her seven sons (martyrs; unnamed in text, named in tradition as Hannah or Miriam)

2 Maccabees

- The mother and her seven sons (see above)

Susanna

- Susanna — Daniel 13 (in some canons)

Bel and the Dragon

- (No named women)

Prayer of Manasseh

- (No named women)

1 Esdras

- (No named women)

2 Esdras

- (No named women)

Prayer of Azariah

- (No named women)

THE GOSPELS

Matthew

- Tamar — Matthew 1:3 (see Genesis)

- Rahab — Matthew 1:5 (see Joshua)

- Ruth — Matthew 1:5 (see Ruth)

- Bathsheba (as "wife of Uriah") — Matthew 1:6 (see 2 Samuel)

- Mary (mother of Jesus) — Matthew 1–2; 12:46–50; 13:55; 27:56–61; 28:1–10

- Elizabeth — Luke 1 (see Luke)

- Herodias — Matthew 14:3–11; Mark 6:17–28; Luke 3:19

- Herodias's daughter (Salome; named in tradition) — Matthew 14:6–11; Mark 6:22–28

- The Canaanite woman (Syrophoenician woman) — Matthew 15:21–28; Mark 7:24–30

- Mary Magdalene — Matthew 27:56–61; 28:1–10; Mark 15:40–47; 16:1–11; Luke 8:2; 24:10; John 19:25; 20:1–18

- Mary of James (mother of James and Joseph) — Matthew 27:56; Mark 15:40; 16:1; Luke 24:10

- The mother of the sons of Zebedee (Salome, according to Mark) — Matthew 20:20–28; 27:56

185

Mark

- Salome — Mark 15:40; 16:1
- Herodias (see Matthew)
- Herodias's daughter (see Matthew)
- The Syrophoenician woman (see Matthew)
- Mary Magdalene (see Matthew)
- Mary of James (see Matthew)
- Salome (see above)
- The widow who gave two mites — Mark 12:41–44; Luke 21:1–4

Luke

- Elizabeth — Luke 1
- Mary (mother of Jesus) — Luke 1–2; see Matthew
- Anna (prophetess) — Luke 2:36–38
- Joanna — Luke 8:3; 24:10
- Susanna — Luke 8:3
- Mary Magdalene (see Matthew)
- Martha — Luke 10:38–42; John 11–12
- Mary of Bethany — Luke 10:38–42; John 11–12
- The sinful woman (who anointed Jesus) — Luke 7:36–50
- The woman with the hemorrhage — Luke 8:43–48; Matthew 9:20–22; Mark 5:25–34
- The widow of Nain — Luke 7:11–17
- The woman bent over for eighteen years — Luke 13:10–17
- Herodias (see Matthew)
- Joanna (see above)
- Mary of James (see Matthew)
- The daughters of Jerusalem (on the via dolorosa) — Luke 23:27–31
- The women at the empty tomb (collective) — Luke 24:1–12

John

- Mary (mother of Jesus) — John 2:1–12; 19:25–27
- The Samaritan woman — John 4
- Martha — John 11–12 (see Luke)

- Mary of Bethany — John 11–12 (see Luke)
- The woman caught in adultery — John 7:53–8:11
- Mary Magdalene — John 19:25; 20:1–18 (see Matthew)
- Mary of Clopas — John 19:25
- Salome (implied in "his mother's sister") — John 19:25
- The mother of the sons of Zebedee (see Matthew, Mark)

THE ACTS OF THE APOSTLES

- Mary (mother of Jesus) — Acts 1:14
- Mary Magdalene (implied in upper room? Not named)
- The women disciples (collective) — Acts 1:14
- Sapphira — Acts 5:1–11
- Tabitha (Dorcas) — Acts 9:36–42
- Rhoda — Acts 12:12–17
- Mary (mother of John Mark) — Acts 12:12–17
- Lydia — Acts 16:14–15, 40
- The slave girl with a spirit of divination — Acts 16:16–18
- Damaris — Acts 17:34
- Priscilla (Prisca) — Acts 18; Romans 16:3; 1 Corinthians 16:19; 2 Timothy 4:19
- Philip's daughters (four unmarried prophetesses) — Acts 21:9
- Bernice — Acts 25:13–23; 26:30
- Drusilla — Acts 24:24

THE EPISTLES

Romans
- Phoebe — Romans 16:1–2
- Prisca (Priscilla) — Romans 16:3–4 (see Acts)
- Mary (of Rome) — Romans 16:6
- Junia — Romans 16:7
- Tryphaena — Romans 16:12

- Tryphosa — Romans 16:12
- Persis — Romans 16:12
- Rufus's mother — Romans 16:13
- Julia — Romans 16:15
- Nereus's sister — Romans 16:15
- Olympas — Romans 16:15 (possibly feminine)

1 Corinthians
- Chloe — 1 Corinthians 1:11
- Prisca (Priscilla) — 1 Corinthians 16:19 (see Acts)

2 Corinthians
- (No named women)

Galatians
- (No named women)

Ephesians
- (No named women)

Philippians
- Euodia — Philippians 4:2
- Syntyche — Philippians 4:2
- Clement's female coworkers (unnamed, but implied) — Philippians 4:3

Colossians
- (No named women; Nympha may be feminine in some manuscripts)
- Nympha — Colossians 4:15 (feminine in some manuscripts; masculine in others)

1 Thessalonians
- (No named women)

2 Thessalonians
- (No named women)

1 Timothy

- Eunice — 2 Timothy 1:5 (see 2 Timothy)
- Lois — 2 Timothy 1:5 (see 2 Timothy)

2 Timothy

- Eunice — 2 Timothy 1:5
- Lois — 2 Timothy 1:5
- Claudia — 2 Timothy 4:21
- Prisca (Priscilla) — 2 Timothy 4:19 (see Acts)

Titus

- (No named women)

Philemon

- Apphia — Philemon 1:2

Hebrews

- Sarah — Hebrews 11:11 (see Genesis)
- Rahab — Hebrews 11:31 (see Joshua)
- Jochebed (implied in Moses' parents) — Hebrews 11:23

James

- (No named women)

1 Peter

- Sarah — 1 Peter 3:6 (see Genesis)

2 Peter

- (No named women)

1 John

- The elect lady — 2 John 1:1 (possibly symbolic or literal)
- The elect sister's children — 2 John 1:13

2 John

- The elect lady — 2 John 1:1 (see above)

3 John

- (No named women)

Jude

- (No named women)

REVELATION

- Jezebel (of Thyatira) — Revelation 2:20–23
- The woman clothed with the sun — Revelation 12
- The Bride (the New Jerusalem; personified) — Revelation 19:7–9; 21:2, 9–10
- The great prostitute (Babylon; personified) — Revelation 17–18

APPENDIX: WOMEN KNOWN ONLY BY RELATIONSHIP

This index would be incomplete without acknowledging the many women whose names are not recorded but whose stories are preserved. These include:

- Lot's wife (Genesis 19)
- Job's wife (Job 2)
- Samson's mother (Judges 13)
- Jephthah's daughter (Judges 11)
- The medium of En-dor (1 Samuel 28)
- The wise woman of Tekoa (2 Samuel 14)
- The widow of Zarephath (1 Kings 17)
- The Shunammite woman (2 Kings 4, 8)
- Naaman's servant girl (2 Kings 5)
- The woman with the hemorrhage (Matthew 9; Mark 5; Luke 8)
- The Syrophoenician woman (Matthew 15; Mark 7)

- The Samaritan woman (John 4)
- The woman caught in adultery (John 8)
- Philip's four daughters (Acts 21)
- And countless others whose names are known only to God

"Blessed are those who wash their robes, so that they may have the right to the tree of life and that they may enter the city by the gates." — Revelation 22:14

BIBLIOGRAPHY

Calpino, Teresa. "Tabitha and Lydia—Models of Early Christian Women Leaders." Biblical Archaeology Review, July/August 2016.

Cartlidge, David R. "Thecla: The Apostle Who Defied Women's Destiny." *Bible Review*, December 2004.

Hylen, Susan E. Women in the New Testament World. New York: Oxford University Press, 2019.

Lightfoot, J.B. Philippians. 4th ed. London, 1878.

Muir, Elizabeth Gillan. A Women's History of the Christian Church: Two Thousand Years of Female Leadership. Toronto: University of Toronto Press, 2019.

Schaberg, Jane. "How Mary Magdalene Became a Whore." Bible Review, October 1992.

Witherington, Ben, III. "Joanna: Apostle of the Lord or Jailbait?" Bible Review, Spring 2005.

Witherington, Ben, III. Women in the Earliest Churches. Cambridge: Cambridge University Press, 1988.

Zamfir, Korinna, and Uta Poplutz, eds. Reading Women in the New Testament Letters. Atlanta: SBL Press, 2025.

ABOUT THE AUTHOR

Colin Wallace is a father of three and lives in Toronto, Ontario, Canada. I wish I had such a book when I named by children, so I researched and wrote this book. I hope it informs your decision. Please leave a review and if you choose a name from this book leave it in the review.